Language Learners and their Errors

by John Norrish

Essential Language Teaching Series

General Editor: Roger H Flavell

Macmillan Press London

First published 1983

Published by
THE MACMILLAN PRESS LIMITED
London and Basingstoke
Associated companies throughout the world

ISBN 0 333 27180 7

Printed in Hong Kong

Acknowledgements

I should like to thank all those who, at various times and in different places, have helped with the completion of this book. My colleagues in the ESOL Department at the Institute of Education and several generations of students deserve special mention. Two names in particular I would like to single out: Roger Flavell, the series editor and my colleague, for spending many hours in patient discussion, and Deborah Tyler for doing such an efficient editing job on the manuscript.

Dedication

To my Parents

The author and publishers wish to thank the following who have kindly given permission for the use of copyright material:-

Cambridge University Press for an extract from *Communicate* by Morrow and Johnson, and an adapted table from *101 Substitution Tables for Students of English* by H V George.

K G Kyei for the poem "I No be Like You" from *No Time to Die* by K G Kyei and H Schreckenbach.

Liber Grafiska AB for two tables adapted from an article "The Effects of Different Types of Errors in the Communication System" by M Olsson, in *Errata* edited by J Svartvik.

Oxford University Press for tables from *A Guide to Patterns and Usage in English* by A S Hornby (1st edition 1954); an extract from *English Topics* by V J Cook (c) Vivian Cook 1974, and an extract from *Reading and Thinking in English, Discovery Discourse* (c) The British Council 1979.

Times Newspapers Limited for a cartoon by Dutton in *100 of the Best* published by Penguin Books Ltd. for The Times Education Supplement, 1968

University of Cambridge Local Examinations Syndicate for four questions from First Certificate Paper 5, June 1979.

Preface

Why are mistakes such a common feature of the language teacher's and language learner's life? Are mistakes made because of lack of attention, or is there more to it than that? Pages covered with red ink are disheartening to the student who has put hours of effort into the exercise and mean extra work for the teacher. Can, or should, the teacher help students to make fewer mistakes? These are some of the questions dealt with in this book. I should point out that I make no claims to having found the answer to all of them, but I hope this book will make the role of the mistake in language-learning clear, as well as providing suggestions for how to deal with mistakes.

There may be no simple way of preventing all mistakes but I do not think that matters. What is more important is realising that making mistakes can be a necessary and useful part of the learning process. I hope this book will help language teachers to change their attitude to students' mistakes and see them in a more positive way, rather than as signs of failure on the teacher's or student's part.

This book will bring the reader up-to-date with current thinking on errors in language learning. It is intended to be read right through rather than dipped into for reference. Summaries are provided at the end of each chapter and linguistic terms are explained in the Glossary on page 126.

Contents

1 Errors; attitudes and principles

There are basically two different attitudes to mistakes or errors made by people learning languages other than their own. (See page 7 for a discussion of the different types of 'mistakes'.) Probably most teachers regard mistakes as undesirable, a sign of failure either on the students' part to pay attention or 'to listen properly', or else on the teacher's part to make his meaning clear or to give the students sufficient time to 'practise' what they have been taught. But on the other hand there is an Italian proverb *Sbagliando s'impara* (We learn through our errors) and making mistakes can indeed be regarded as an essential part of learning.

1.1 Errors as failure

INHIBITION
In many traditional language classes students have been made to feel that errors bring discredit on the teacher and learner alike and have been reprimanded for making too many errors. This implies that errors are the fault of the student and could be avoided.

Many people will agree that one of the most inhibiting factors in any formal learning situation is the fear of making mistakes and being thought ridiculous either by native speakers, one's classmates or by the teacher. This leads to the characteristic hesitancy among learners to say anything in a foreign language for fear of appearing a fool. This form of behaviour has been described by Earl Stevick (1976:40 *et passim*) as 'defensive learning'. The learner is not so much concerned with attempting to express what he would like to say, either orally or in writing, as rather with saying what he thinks he can without making mistakes. The actual substance of the message is relegated to second place while the learner concentrates on the 'correct' form of what he is trying to say. 'Will I get the accent right?' 'Is that the right pronoun for that place?' As anyone who has broken through this barrier will have discovered, there is seldom one right form in any case; there is much more likely to be a number of alternatives (see page 5 for some practical examples of this point). But how many of us as teachers can honestly say that we have encouraged our students to experiment and to think of alternative ways of putting what they want to say?

LANGUAGE-TEACHING METHODOLOGY

How often does one hear the statement 'I'm bad at languages'? And yet everybody in the world has learnt one language very well: his or her own. If we can all learn a language as infants but find second language learning so difficult, then maybe it is the teaching methods that are at fault.

Aims

The language teacher's attitude to errors is influenced by his view of what he is trying to do in class. In apparently punishing error, what is the teacher hoping to achieve? Few would wish to disagree that a painstaking attitude to learning and a desire to produce only the best work and settle for nothing less than perfect is an admirable general educational aim. But is this the most appropriate target in language teaching? There is an immediate and obvious difference between teaching languages and a subject such as Geography, although this has often been forgotten in the language classroom: language isn't a set of facts to be learned but a medium for expressing thoughts, feelings and communicating with other people.

It is true that many have learnt languages by a method that has regarded language teaching as very similar to teaching any academic subject and some learners may even be able to use language learnt this way. But the majority of language learners only acquire an *active* knowledge of the language if they have the opportunity to listen to a great deal of the language and to make numerous mistakes while expressing themselves in it. The language learner will find that he is more successful in getting his message across in the foreign language if he speaks reasonably quickly and makes some mistakes rather than hesitating before every word he is not certain about. In other words, what may be more highly valued in speech in real life is 'fluency' rather than a somewhat academic accuracy. The point here, then, is that drawing the learner's attention to every mistake he makes, encouraging him to be aware of these mistakes, and making him think at length before speaking or writing, may not help him to use the language in the most natural or useful way.

'But what of the exam?' teachers may say. There are two points to be mentioned here. First, accuracy is *not* being thrown out of the window; if there are too many grammatical mistakes, the listener may not be able to understand the message, however fluently it is delivered. The second point is that teachers can encourage their students to attempt fluency with the limited amount of the language they have. Even elementary students with a very limited stock of structures and vocabulary can take part in activities which encourage use of the language that has been learnt, such as finding another student with a similar card in a card-matching game. (See Revell 1979 and Rixon 1981 in this series for useful ideas.)

Correcting errors
Activities practising newly taught language, such as the card-matching game mentioned above, take place in a relatively lifelike situation and teachers can note mistakes as they occur. The implication for methodology here is clear: there are times when pointing out mistakes and thereby interrupting the flow of an activity could be counterproductive. It is possible to note the mistakes and deal with them at a more suitable time (see also page 50). The advantages of

this approach are that, firstly, students do not become over-aware of making mistakes but regard the language as a tool for expression and, secondly, both the students and the teacher see the language that has been taught put into practice immediately. The students are motivated by the need for the language they are learning and the teacher has evidence of the students' ability to use the language.

It is worth saying, for teachers who feel that this approach to mistakes is too risky when it comes to preparing students for an exam, that students are more likely to develop a feel for the language through using it in a meaningful context than by doing corrections three times over. The very common idea that by writing a correct form three (or more) times a student will learn it, is not only seen to be ineffective by almost any teacher with any class, but is also based on a theory of learning that is no longer commonly held to be true. This behaviourist view of language learning as primarily a matter of habit formation (ie if the learner does something often enough, regardless of whether he is paying attention to what he is doing or not, the correct habit will be formed) is no longer as common as it used to be because much of the recent work in the field has shown that such a notion is a gross over-simplication (see Stevick 1976, de Villiers and de Villiers 1979 and the sources mentioned in them).

What language to teach

Sometimes teachers are over-conscious of students' mistakes because of an entirely praiseworthy desire to teach the best possible form of the language. The problem lies in deciding what the 'best' form is. In English, for example, contractions (eg I'm, can't, won't, etc) are sometimes held to be lazy speech and should be treated as mistakes if the student uses them. This is a dubious procedure for at least two reasons. First, if the teacher treats as a mistake forms which are often produced by native speakers of the target language (see the Glossary on page 126 for definitions of linguistic terms), the learner will become confused. A teacher's best goal is to get his students to do what native speakers do. As contractions are very frequent in

English speech, it is sensible to allow students to use them. Second, research into the kinds of language used in different situations by native speakers has shown that the 'best' form will depend on what is appropriate for the situation.

The idea that a formal, written style is 'the best' is a widely held misconception. In an informal conversation between a husband and wife, the following utterance is not at all likely: 'With whom did you have lunch, darling?' Anyone who spoke like this instead of saying: 'Who did you have lunch with?' would sound like a rather inflexible and unbending kind of character. In the context of a public lecture, however, a speaker is more likely to use a form like 'the statement with which I began my talk...' than 'the statement I began my talk with...' The native speaker builds up, in the course of all his different contacts with his language in a variety of different situations, an almost unconscious knowledge of which forms to use where. Clearly, this knowledge will depend to a certain extent on his experience of the different situations in question; without this, a speaker may inadvertently produce an inappropriate form and even on occasion an 'overcorrected form' (eg 'the man with whom I came in with') in trying to make his speech formal to match an unaccustomed situation.

The important point for the language teacher is that it can be misleading to call an informal form a mistake, and if the form is used in a situation where a native speaker would also use an informal expression then it is quite wrong to penalise the student. What the teacher needs to point out is precisely that certain forms are more likely to occur in certain situations. No one variety of language is the 'best'. Students must be equipped with the spoken or written variety or varieties of language they are most likely to need. Correcting of mistakes then takes the form of pointing out inappropriate use of language. For example, in such basic areas as greetings, students should be aware of the differences between 'Good morning', 'Hello' and 'Hi'. Over-use of the more formal 'Good morning' would be as inappropriate as the use of 'Hi' in the wrong circumstances.

Classroom activities

Allowing students to perform dramatic activities in the classroom, culminating in role-play, will enable them to appreciate the relation of certain kinds of language to certain situations. It must be stressed, however, that this needs very careful preparation, both physical and linguistic. The physical preparation of the classroom will involve moving furniture, where possible and appropriate, to allow free movement. Desks and chairs in usual places tend to restrain the free movement needed for any kind of dramatic classroom re-creation of outside situations. Space is essential for movement. The linguistic preparation will involve presenting appropriate linguistic items for the particular situation. In a role-play, for example of a radio station going on the air for a news programme, the language needed would almost certainly be more formal than that required for an animated discussion between two car drivers involved in a minor traffic accident. (See Revell 1979 for practical suggestions for role-play.)

An important reason for encouraging freer types of language activity in the classroom is this: what the teacher teaches is not always the same as what the learner learns. Indeed, teaching would be simpler if it were. Much recent research has indicated (especially Krashen 1981) that language learners find it easier to use the language they are learning if it is practised in precisely these uncontrolled situations, where the learner is more concerned with achieving something through language than with 'getting the answer right'.

1.2 Errors as positive aids to learning

Some good pedagogical reasons have been suggested for regarding errors made by learners of a foreign language leniently but the most important reason is that the error itself may actually be a *necessary* part of learning a language.

FIRST LANGUAGE ACQUISITION

There has been a great deal of research in the field of first language acquisition. (A good introduction to the study of how people learn to use their mother tongue is de Villiers and de Villiers 1979.) One thing which now seems quite clear is that at some stages of learning their mother tongue, children make guesses about the forms of their language and these guesses are based on the information that they already have about the language. For example, most children growing up and learning English as their mother tongue produce the form 'goed' at some stage for 'went'. Now this, viewed from the perspective of adult grammar, can be called a mistake: it is not the form that an adult or older child would use. However, it can also be regarded as an informed guess, based on the observation that in English the simple past tense is formed in the majority of cases with -ed. (The child could not describe what he was doing in these terms, of course, but observation of his language behaviour would lead to this conclusion.)

DIFFERENT TYPES OF 'ERROR'

It would be useful at this stage to distinguish between different types of anomalous language behaviour: the error, the mistake and the lapse. Let us call a systematic deviation, when a learner has not learnt something and consistently 'gets it wrong', an **error**. As mentioned above, a child aquiring his own language sometimes consistently makes the same error. In the same way, when a learner of English as a second or foreign language makes an error systematically, it is because he has not learnt the correct form. A common example is using the infinitive with 'to' after the verb 'must' (eg 'I must to go to the shops'). Let us suppose that the learner knows the verbs want (+ to), need (+ to) and perhaps ought (+ to); by analogy he then produces must (+ to). Until he has been told otherwise, or until he notices that native speakers do not produce this form, he will say or write this quite consistently.

Once a learner has noticed or been taught that in English the verb 'must' does not follow the same pattern as some of the other modal verbs, there may well be a period during which he produces 'he must go' *and* ' he must to go'. Sometimes he will use one form and sometimes the other, quite inconsistently. This inconsistent deviation we shall call a **mistake**: sometimes the learner 'gets it right' but sometimes he makes a mistake and uses the wrong form.

There is another type of wrong usage which is neither a mistake nor an error and can happen to anyone at any time. This is a **lapse**, which may be due to lack of concentration, shortness of memory, fatigue, etc. A lapse bears little relation to whether or not a given form in the language has been learnt, has not been learnt or is in the process of being learnt. Native speakers suffer lapses in the same way as learners of the language; a recent example was a presenter of BBC's Radio 4 who said 'chieving to astrive' instead of 'striving to achieve'.

Many teachers may feel that there is another type of common 'mistake': a **careless slip**, caused by the learner's inattentiveness in class. In fact, by referring to any kind of unacceptable or inappropriate form as 'careless' we are pre-judging the cause and blaming the learner for it. To be realistic, we must admit that classrooms are not always populated by the ideal, motivated, attentive students we would hope for. But can we call a learner careless who produces the following utterance: 'That is the man that I saw him last Friday' after he has worked at sentences demonstrating relative clauses? Clearly there are many possible explanations for this deviation and we are denying ourselves the chance of valuable insights into what is going on in the learner's mind if we ascribe this behaviour to simple carelessness.

Summary

The development of the ability to express oneself in a new language is one of the most interesting areas of human study and this book sets out to clarify some of the issues in this field.

The main purpose of this first chapter has been to persuade teachers to treat learners' shortcomings more leniently and to help learners gain a sense of enjoyment and confidence in using the new language.

The points made in this chapter are:

1   One of the most inhibiting factors in learning and using a foreign language is the fear of appearing ridiculous by making mistakes.

2   Too much importance is often attached by teachers to mistakes, as a result of a rather academic approach to the subject which ignores what we now know of the complex task of language learning.

3   Fluency is as important an aim in language-teaching as knowledge of correct forms.

4   *Inappropriate* forms can be just as 'wrong' as *unacceptable* ones, hence the value of putting language into situations with the help of role-plays, etc.

5   The errors made by the child learning his mother tongue and by the foreign language learner can be regarded as actual evidence of the learning of a system (though the learner's system is not yet the same as that of the standard language) having taken place.

2   Psychology of learning

2.1   Native speaker and foreign learner errors

One of the main differences between the learner and the native speaker of a language is that the native speaker, if he does deviate from the norm, can correct himself.

L_1 speakers commonly make small slips when they are speaking, such as the lack of subject/verb agreement in this piece of transcribed speech: 'Yes er *they*, as I was saying yesterday I think, quite definitely *was* the best holiday we ever had'. But if a tape is made of the speaker's conversation and played back to him, he will be able to correct himself. However, a learner who has learnt that 'any' is used in question forms will not realise what is wrong with saying 'Please could you give me any bread?' in a restaurant for example, unless the distinction between *questions* and *requests* with 'some' and 'any' was pointed out to him.

The other main difference between the L_1 speaker and the L_2 learner is that the learner already knows another language. Interference from this language is often considered one of the most frequent causes of error. This topic will be treated in more detail in Chapter 3.

RELATION OF FIRST AND SECOND LANGUAGE LEARNING
It was pointed out in Chapter 1 that children learning their first language tend to produce forms which are, if we view them by the standards of an adult's grammar, deviant. These were referred to as 'informed guesses' which would subsequently be adjusted in the light of further information. What we have said, in essence, is that these

errors are a necessary part of a child's learning activities while he acquires his first language.

There is now a considerable body of opinion which claims that the strategies used by someone learning a second language are, if not the same as then very similar to, those used by the first language learner (Dulay and Burt 1974; Hatch 1978). This should not be misunderstood as meaning that the two activities are 'the same'; rather that the foreign language learner's systematic handling of the data to which he has been exposed will have certain characteristics in common with first language learning. So it appears that not only is the error an inevitable part of the learner's output but it is quite possibly a necessary part too. Deviations provide useful information for the teacher, helping the teacher to plot the learning activity as it takes place.

2.2 Performance Analysis

It is self-evident that language learning takes place over a period of time and at any one time in this period the learner will produce some forms correctly, some incorrectly and others inconsistently. But how can noting a student's errors tell us about what he *knows* of the target language as opposed to what he actually *does*?

Generally, teachers consider a learner's output in terms of deviation from the native speaker's output. To put it another way, the learner is judged by the mistakes he produces, not the correct forms. An alternative to this would be to regard the learner's output as indicating a 'staging post', a sign of where he is on the journey from complete ignorance of the target language to a competent command of it. This stage of development is more reliably gauged by looking at what the learner knows, or gets right, as well as what he doesn't know.

The transitional stage of the learner's development has been referred to variously by different writers on the subject as 'interlanguage' (Selinker 1972), 'approximative systems' (Nemser 1971), 'interlingua' (James 1971) and 'idiosyncratic dialect' (Corder 1971). One advantage of 'performance analysis' (Corder 1975), looking not only at deviations but also at current forms to determine the learner's progress, is that the teacher can gain a clearer overall picture of what the student knows, his transitional competence, and not simply of what mistakes are being made. (See Figure 1 for an example of a simple performance analysis.) As any learner knows, it is much more satisfactory to have recognition for getting answers right than only to have one's mistakes commented upon. This performance analysis allows more individual treatment to be given to students. Records can be kept, indicating in broad outline what the student knows and what he has not yet learned. However, if *all* the students in a class are making *different* random mistakes, then there must be something wrong with the teaching plan for the class and the teacher needs to find new material. It is much more likely that there will be common errors. The teacher should compare the performance analyses of all the students in the class and then plan remedial work.

A teacher can, over the years, build up a battery of exercises on various teaching points, or can at least build up a list of exercises in textbooks which are readily available. From this stock of exercises, the teacher can choose work that is better suited to the individual student's particular stage of development. In many classes, there is some small amount of time each week when this kind of work can be done.

2.3 Sources of error

In trying to analyse the reasons for errors being made it is important to notice the distinction between teaching and learning. As many teachers know all too well, what the teacher teaches is not by any means always the same as what the learner learns. It would be wrong of teachers to attribute this to lack of attention to the teaching material. True, this may be the case, but it is quite clearly not always so.

Errors may arise from the choice of the material itself; from its teaching points being presented in a certain order; from the ordering

What we did (yesterday) on our outing

Yesterday we had a outing for school.
On eight o'clock we drived to the lake.
The whater was beautiful.
We went to the second lake.
Then we ate our bread and drank our lemonade.
Later we went to the first lake.
Then we ate in the Restaurant our pomes frites and our sausage.
Later we played in the park for the Restaurant with the ball
                                    then we went to the bus and drived to home. In Gunskirchen they all went home. they outing was really beautiful.

<u>article</u> : a outing <u>they</u> outing	X ("wrong") spelling: whater (= water) pomes frites

<u>preposition</u>: an outing for school
    ....the park <u>for</u> the restaurant
    ...<u>on</u> 8 o'clock
    <u>to</u> home
	— <u>word order</u>
	... ate in the restaurant our..

<u>past tense</u>: drived (X 2)	

	V ("right")
<u>past tense</u>:	had, was, went, ate, played
<u>spelling</u>:	beautiful, yesterday, outing, lemonade

Figure 1   Example of simple performance analysis

of the examples of the language; as a result of the practice work accompanying the examples, or from the learner's processing of these materials. For example, if the present continuous tense is taught early on in a course, there may well be a tendency to over-use it. Captions to illustrations can also lead to the mis-use of tenses, such as the use in Figure 2 of the present simple, where the continuous tense would be less misleading.

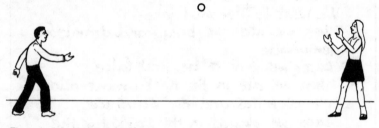

Figure 2   John throws the ball.

Even if an attentive student has a good teacher who presents a teaching point from the target language in the clearest way he can and follows it with plenty of opportunity for the student to practise the item(s) concerned, we cannot say after each lesson that learning has taken place. This is, of course, true in any subject, but in language learning it is especially so.

As Corder remarks, language is a system of systems, with all parts being interconnected, therefore, nothing can be 'fully learned' until all the parts are fully learned. What we try to do as teachers, then, is to allow our students to learn the rule systems of the target language by presenting them with sentences which exemplify the rules so as to develop a competence in the language as a whole. Obviously this is only part of the story, since we also want our students to be aware of the situations in which utterances are used, but however much time is devoted in class to a communicative style of teaching (see Revell 1979), the chances of success will be small unless the language data presented to the students are such as to allow them to build up (not necessarily consciously) rules of production and use.

All the reasons for errors given on page 1 except the last one (the learner's processing of the materials), are within the teacher's control to change. That is, they are all part of the activities associated with the teaching process. The last factor is not within the teacher's control, nor yet within the student's own control, and has been classified as part of human psychology by one writer (Corder 1973:283).

A group of factors influencing learning ability with which most teachers would be familiar are the personal ones, involving the student's state of mind. A student may be in a particularly good mood or be distracted by things that concern him outside the classroom. These personal factors may lead to unnecessary mistakes. They have been referred to by Corder as 'redundant' and are clearly different from the error which arises specifically from the language-learning activity (ie the 'inherent' error which may be a necessary part of learning a language).

For example, a German learner of English may place the verb in a subordinate clause at the end of the clause, because he has not yet learnt that in English, unlike German, this is not usually done. This would be an 'inherent' error. But if the same student, having learnt this fact of English grammar, then regresses and makes the same error again because he is worrying about some personal problem, his error would then be a redundant error.

'How's the sleep learning progressing, Harper?'

Figure 3   Formation of redundant errors - *TES, 100 of the best.*

An awareness of these personal factors may be useful to the teacher in helping the student to make the most of his abilities.

DIFFERENT LEARNING STRATEGIES

It can be seen in the work of any language class that, even given an identical input, the resulting errors and mistakes are not identical. A fairly superficial examination of students' performance would bear this out. While some students make multiple errors in a particular language system and suddenly move to 'correct' forms, others move more gradually, item by item. Some students appear to learn in a linear progression, others apparently adopt a different procedure and seem to move by flashes of insight whereby whole 'chunks' of the language system are learned. This does not necessarily mean that this is a conscious activity; in some cases it may be, but in many it is clearly beyond the control of the learner himself.

The implication for the teacher in the fact that students have very different ways of learning the material that is presented to them is the need for individualisation. This is true in all kinds of learning but especially so in language-learning. If a student is to learn as efficiently as possible, then the teaching techniques need to be adapted to his individual learning strategies, as far as this is possible in class teaching.

The errors we have been looking at so far, by implication at least, have been syntactic rather than phonological (ie concerned with grammar rather than pronunciation). But before we look at the particular problems of pronunciation, we should mention one other category of error: lexical error.

Lexical error

Lexis forms a potentially open set of items, with new words being introduced as and when the need arises, whereas the phonological and syntactic systems are closed and, despite a certain shift in phonology in most languages, relatively unchanging over the short term. As far as the effective learning of lexis is concerned, the introduction of new vocabulary in context and *when the need arises* has been found to be the most efficient aid to learning. Pronunciation, however, presents different problems and needs different procedures.

PSYCHOLOGY OF PRONUNCIATION ERRORS

Interference from first language

Although the habit formation theory of language acquisition is no longer held to be true, much of what the learner does *in the field of pronunciation* is demonstrably a matter of habit. The vocal organs, moving very much faster than we could consciously tell them to, become accustomed to dividing up the available spaces in the vocal tract in a certain way. The sounds in any one language form a system and someone listening to a language other than his own will tend to 'hear' the sounds of his own language, or at least sounds close to those of his own language, rather than those that are, in fact, being produced in the foreign language. For example, many learners of English have trouble distinguishing between the vowel sounds in 'hit' and 'heat' because although the difference is significant in English it isn't in many other languages.

The same can be said of stress patterns. Many languages have stressed syllables at roughly equal distances in time which are not dependent on the number of unstressed syllables in between. They are called *stress-timed* languages. English is one of these languages. Consider the following:

The 'man is 'here
The 'Mansion House is 'here.

Both of these sentences would take a roughly similar time for a native English speaker to utter because the different syllables would be pronounced at different speeds. In some other languages each syllable occupies roughly the same amount of time. These are called *syllable-timed* languages. To a speaker of a stress-timed language, a syllable-timed language will sound like a machine gun. English, on the other hand, would sound slurred and slovenly to a speaker of a syllable-timed language.

The point here is that it is very easy for a teacher who is proficient in the target language to forget just how 'foreign' it can sound to a rather new learner.

Accent

Expecting learners to produce these sounds — often reported by the learners as 'funny' — is in effect expecting them to give up part of their familiar selves. At certain ages, notably adolescence, there will be a strong tendency to avoid making oneself 'look silly' in the eyes of one's friends; making these 'strange sounds' successfully could well have that effect. By apparently wishing to join another group, the adolescent could mark himself off from his peers and from his own national group. To a lesser extent, this is true of some adults, too. It may well be, then, that teachers should be prepared to tolerate imperfections in pronunciation in learners.

This is not, as it may seem, suggesting a radical decline in 'standards', but rather that some priorities should be allowed to shift a little. It is well known that a foreign accent, provided it is not so heavy as to obscure the message, can sound rather attractive to native speakers.

It is also difficult to be dogmatic about pronunciation when an exceptionally large number of dialects are spoken in the British Isles alone. The teacher who insists that the pronunciation pattern of one of the many varieties of English spoken as a mother tongue throughout the world is the only acceptable version of English phonology is creating unnecessary problems for his students. In an environment where English is spoken as a second language, there may be disadvantages in having a recognisable 'English' or 'American' accent. For learners of English as a foreign language it may simplify the learning considerably if the sounds are selected on the basis of those which are closest to the mother tongue and therefore easiest for the learners (see Valdman 1975).

Motivation

Research indicates that there are two basic types of motivation in language-learning: integrative and instrumental. The former, often giving rise to more satisfactory performance in the target language, relates to the learner's willingness to identify with the culture, perceived personality and habits of the speakers of the language. The latter type of motivation (producing, it is claimed, less satisfactory results) is seen in the learner who wishes not so much to integrate in any way with speakers of the language, but rather to use the language for a specific purpose, say, for study or business reasons. More phonological errors are likely to be found in a class whose motivation is primarily of the second type.

Sociology

There may be sociological factors that affect the learner's type of motivation. In environments where English, for example, is used instrumentally as an official language and a *lingua franca*, the 'standard' form of the language as taught in the classroom will have competition from the forms used in contexts outside the school. Both syntax and phonology may differ considerably here, since there are strong social and perhaps political reasons for expressing solidarity with one's own group rather than the group who speak the language as a mother tongue. In Ghana, for example, some Ghanaians may think that one of their compatriates who speaks English with a clearly identifiable British public school accent is trying to imitate the former colonial model. Shortcomings in pronunciation in such circumstances cannot be explained by referring to so-called lazy tongues and lethargic muscles. The teacher needs a sensitive attitude to what at first may have seemed to be a perverse unwillingness to make the necessary adjustment even after clear demonstration and/or explanation. Psychology of error blends imperceptibly with sociology in this area. (This will be developed further in Chapter 3.)

Summary

Native speakers make lapses when using their own language but these are different from the errors made by foreign learners. In learning a foreign language the learner is influenced by his first language (this may lead to mistakes in both syntax and pronunciation) but there are other psychological factors affecting the learner.

1 The learner does not necessarily learn what the teacher thinks he is teaching, since the learner processes the data presented to him by the teacher in his own way. This may be partly determined by the learner's cultural background, his previous learning experience, his aptitude for languages, his attitude to those who speak the target language, and his age.
2 Students have different learning strategies which respond to different teaching techniques.
3 Personal factors outside the classroom may cause the learner to make redundant errors.
4 The learner's motivation may be integrative or instrumental.
5 Pronunciation errors may relate to the learner's personality and a reluctance (perhaps for sociological or political reasons) to identify with the native speakers of the new language by acquiring their accent.

The language teacher needs to be aware of all these possible factors and be sympathetic towards the learner's problems. An analysis of each student's performance, both in terms of what he does know and what he doesn't know, will help show the teacher how that student goes about learning the language.

Language is a system of systems and cannot be 'fully learned' until all the interconnected parts are fully learned but 'performance analysis' will help the teacher monitor the student's progress and provide as much individual help as possible.

3   What causes errors?

3.1 Popular ideas

A variety of language teachers, asked what causes errors, will probably come up with similar answers. Some will reply that it is carelessness on the part of the students and others with some linguistic knowledge will usually reply 'first language interference' or 'translation from the first language'. These answers have a measure of truth in them but *only* a measure and do not begin to answer the question fully.

CARELESSNESS
This was discussed in Chapter 2. Carelessness is not the only cause of error, but if a teacher feels that it is possibly a reason for some of his students' errors, he should ask himself: 'Why are some of the students careless?' 'Are they always careless or just sometimes?' 'What are they careless about?'

Carelessness is often closely related to lack of motivation. Many teachers will admit that it is not always the student's fault if he loses interest; perhaps the materials and/or the style of presentation do not suit him.

One way of reducing the number of 'careless' errors in written work is to get students to check each other's work. This will involve students in an active search for errors and English can be used for a genuine communication while discussing these errors in class.

FIRST LANGUAGE INTERFERENCE

It was commonly believed until fairly recently that learning a language (a mother tongue or a foreign language) was a matter of habit formation. The learner's utterances were thought to be gradually 'shaped' towards those of the language he was learning. With the mother tongue, for example, sounds uttered by the young child which resembled those in the mother tongue were 'reinforced' or rewarded by approval of the parents. It was this rewarding, either by increased attention from the parents or by the child's wants being satisfied, which led in turn to repetitions of the utterance and the subsequent formation of linguistic habits.

This is a very brief and somewhat over-simplified account, but it contains the essence of the 'behaviourist' notion of language learning. For a full account of this view of language learning, see Skinner 1957. Skinner's definitive statement of the behaviourist theory of language learning held that if language is essentially a set of habits, then when we try to learn new habits the old ones will interfere with the new ones. This is what is called 'mother tongue interference'. In the classroom the old habits must be drilled out and a new set of responses must be learnt. The notion of mother tongue interference as a main contributor to error in learners' use of foreign languages is related strongly to this particular view of how human beings learn a language.

Linguists have revised their views of language acquisition and learning and now believe, on the basis of a good deal of evidence (see Greene 1975, for a survey of the literature), that we do not simply become conditioned to making responses, but rather form hypotheses about what language is and how it works; the 'rules' (in a descriptive sense) are learnt and modified according to further data from the language to which the learner is exposed. There is even strong evidence that at certain times, if his grammar (the ideas about how his language behaves) is not yet ready, the learner indeed *cannot* repeat what is said to him.

In one of the rare instances where a parent has been heard to 'correct' a child's grammar, the following exchange took place (McNeill 1966:69):

Child Nobody don't like me.
Parent No, say 'nobody likes me'.
Child Nobody don't like me.
(*Eight repetitions of this dialogue*)
Parent No, now listen carefully; say
  'nobody likes me'.
Child Oh! Nobody don't likes me.

What was true of this case may be true of learners at certain stages of their progress towards the target language, and at times learners may be simply unable to reproduce the 'correct ' form.

There are clearly some differences between a child learning his first language and the student in the classroom. The main difference is that in many classes the teacher has to help as many students as possible to develop sufficient competence in the language to pass an exam or test. The question then raises itself as to how teachers should deal with deviations which appear to be due to L_1 transfer or to any other cause. The answer is that there is no special technique or set of techniques. Since students all learn in different ways, the best thing a teacher can do is to re-teach a given structure, say, or piece of vocabulary, in a way which allows the students to see the language item from as many points of view as possible. It is also important that the learners have a chance to use the item or items in an appropriate situation.

For example, in English 'some' and 'any' are used in different ways. This is quite frequently a source of problems for learners. Here is a suggested procedure for re-teaching the use of 'some' and 'any'.
1 Present 'some' and 'any' in the affirmative and negative with both countables and uncountables. A shop/market scene would be useful here to provide a context. This could take the form of a quick narrative of a shopping expedition or a dialogue, involving two people shopping/searching for different items.

2 Draw up tables, either with the class or write them on the board before the lesson, so the students can see the patterns. (See Figure 4a, b, c and d for examples of suitable tables from Hornby 1954:150 and 151.) Then get students to make up, *quickly*, about ten sentences each. Check the sentences orally in class then perhaps they can be written out as homework.

In this table the nouns are uncountables.

	some no (not) much	(more)		
There is We have	a great deal a good deal a lot lots plenty	more	tea bread sugar	in the storeroom
	a lot of a large quantity of plenty of (not) enough			

Figure 4a

In this table the (pro)nouns are uncountables.

I should like	some no a little a good deal much a lot plenty	more of	this that the brown flour your white flour

Figure 4b

This table illustrates the determinatives used pronominally of countables.

| None
Both
Several
Two or three
Few
A few
Some
Many
A large number
A lot
Lots
All | of | them
these
those | | were broken |
| | | the
these
those
my (your, etc.)
John's | eggs | |

Figure 4c

This table illustrates the determinatives used pronominally of uncountables.

| All
Some
None
Much
A great deal
A good deal
Little
A little
A lot
Lots | of | it
this
that | | is fertile |
| | | this
that
the
our
Mr. Green's | farm land | |

Figure 4d

3   Activity. This can be adapted according to the age and experience of the students.

Give one half of the students shopping list cards and the other half shopkeepers' cards. It helps if the two sets of cards are different colours. The students move round the room and those with the 'shopping lists' try to 'buy' the goods on their list from the shopkeepers. The aim of the game is to cross all the items off the list or sell out all the items in the shop. The activity can be made more complicated by adding prices and a budget, or even, in appropriate environments, bargaining! The language used should include 'Have you any . . . ?' 'I want some . . . please.' 'I haven't got any . . . ' 'Yes, I've got some . . .'

Sample cards

shopping list	shopkeeper
spaghetti	minced beef
minced beef	lamb chops
garlic	liver
tomato puree	kidneys
olive oil	eggs
onion	chicken legs
tomatoes	
mushrooms	
cheese	

TRANSLATION

The third suggestion as to why students make errors is perhaps the most common. Translation word by word of idiomatic expressions in the learner's first language can produce classic howlers. German speakers, for example, may say 'It makes me nothing out' (instead of *I don't mind*), 'Equal goes it loose' (instead of *It's about to start*), or 'The man who I yesterday saw'. Most German speakers of English seem to be well aware of these pitfalls and, indeed, derive much innocent fun from them.

It should be made clear at this point that the distinction between *interference* and *translation* from the first language as causes of student error *is* a fine one. The implication of the term 'interference' is that what takes place is largely unconscious in the mind of the learner. As mentioned on page 22 it was believed that one set of language habits could 'interfere' with the formation of new ones. More recently, however, 'interference' has come to be used in a less technical sense. The original distinction between the two terms is kept here, since it is a useful one (indicating an involuntary strategy on the one hand, but a voluntary one on the other, when students translate as a conscious activity).

Let us consider the possible reasons why a learner may try to translate a familiar expression in his first language into the language he is learning. One of the most typical situations is when a learner has been asked to communicate something, let us say in writing, but is aware that he does not know the appropriate expression or structure. He may even be unaware that an appropriate one exists. Naturally, as he wishes to communicate his ideas, he will fall back on the language system with which he is familiar, namely that of his mother tongue.

Similarly, errors due to translation may occur during a discussion, where students have reached the stage of concentrating more on the *message* (what they want to express) than on the *code* they are using to express it (ie the language). To use rather more technical terminology, the use of conscious or unconscious translation can be regarded as a 'communication strategy', a means whereby a learner can express himself in the language he is learning, using some kind of 'interlanguage' (see page 11) as a half-way house between his own and his target language. As we have already noted, this is surely *not* a phenomenon to be strongly discouraged, since there is now very little evidence indeed that making errors leads to the learning of erroneous forms (see page 22). In any case, this type of activity will not invariably lead to erroneous forms.

Errors such as those made by German speakers cited on page 26 do tend to occur more frequently when translation is used as a teaching/learning activity in class. This may be evidence of the cause of such errors but is not itself an argument against using translation altogether, although translation is probably not the best way of teaching the *use* of a second language.

3.2 Other current theories of the causes of error

CONTRASTIVE ANALYSIS

In 1967 Politzer enthused: 'Perhaps the least questioned and least questionable application of linguistics is the contribution of contrastive analysis.' (For a recent review of the subject, see James 1980.) It was believed that by comparing two linguistic systems, that of the mother tongue and that of the target language, it was possible to predict areas of difficulty, and thus errors. This theory is related to the notion of 'interference' mentioned above. It was found that, contrary to expectations, not all the areas of difference between two language systems actually resulted in errors. Areas where no difficulty had been predicted did produce errors. The main problem with contrastive analysis seems to be that while parts of two language systems may or may not differ, this does not tell us much about how a learner will go about the learning task. Nor does it account for the well-attested fact that the same errors are made by first language speakers from very differing language backgrounds. For example, the learners who made these errors had different backgrounds, one spoke an African language as his mother tongue, the other a European language:

When I reached home, I kiss him.
When the evening came, we go to the pictures.

Teachers who have experience in different countries, or of teaching students with different first languages in the same class, will have noticed that similar errors tend to recur, virtually independently of the students' mother tongue. These errors involving the verb 'to know' were made by different students in a multilingual class:

Does he know to find the way?
Does she know to play hockey?

The other problem, perhaps even greater than the failure of contrastive analysis to predict errors, is the sheer magnitude of the task of writing any contrastive analysis of two languages. In theory you would need as near a complete structural description of both languages as possible. Then, it is necessary actually to contrast the structures. This is no easy task, since it is extremely difficult to devise a consistent system or basis for contrast. For example, look at this English sentence with the Chinese translation underneath. The literal translation of the Chinese is given in italics.

Where is the railway station?
Huo   che   jan   tzai   na   li?
fire   cart   stop   at   which   side

From this sentence it will be noticed that there are a number of structural differences between the two languages. The main one is that there is no verb equivalent in the Chinese sentence for 'is'. Then the two 'words' for 'where' appear at the end of the sentence, not the beginning. And so on and so on . . . It can be seen from this very limited example that to make any kind of contrastive study of two languages is an enormous task, and one, moreover, which has very seldom been carried out. One example of this type of work is Stockwell, Bowen and Martin's well-known work on Spanish and English (Stockwell, Bowen and Martin 1965).

However, for the classroom teacher, contrastive analysis is not entirely without use. Many teachers of English will have a good enough knowledge of the two languages (the students' mother tongue and the target language) to become familiar with certain characteristic errors that the students make, and, if there are any, parallel forms in the mother tongue. A suitable treatment for errors arising from translation from the learners L_1 might, at an intermediate or advanced level, involve pointing out that while in the mother tongue it is possible to say something in this way, nevertheless in the target language it is not. The danger of this approach is that it can lead to an analytical teaching style, which as its prime aim seeks to eliminate certain errors rather than to teach communication through the target language.

Contrastive analysis can, especially in the field of pronunciation, indicate with fair probability certain areas of difficulty. For example, in Thai, some words begin with the *ng* sound, as in English si*ng*. In English this sound does not occur at the beginnings of words. Therefore this might prove a problem for English speakers learning Thai. Note that this is only a possibility; some learners might not find this particularly difficult.

Contrastive analysis can be regarded then by teachers as one of a number of devices in their study of learners' errors. It has its problems, though; the main one being that anyone using the technique needs to know both the mother tongue and the target language and would also need a good grounding in grammar.

GENERAL ORDER OF DIFFICULTY

One interesting idea which is receiving attention from researchers in studying the causes of error is the 'General Order of Difficulty' theory (see Richards and Sampson and work by Ravem, both in Richards 1974). Researchers have found that it is difficult for native speakers as well as for learners of English as a foreign language to distinguish between the English sounds /v/ and /ð/, and /f/ and /θ/. These distinctions are among the last made by English-speaking children learning their mother tongue. As far as structural difficulties are concerned, Carol Chomsky in an investigation of children's control of their mother tongue (English, in this case), between the ages of five and ten years, indicates that even by the age of ten a considerable proportion of children were unable to understand the (apparently) simple structure 'John asked Bill what to do' (Chomsky 1969). She suggests that there is, regardless of the age by which a child has learnt a particular structure, a characteristic order of learning which is almost invariable. This cannot be simply related to the child's need to express a particular concept, or the frequency of use of the structure, as evidence from different languages shows different characteristic orders. Recent work on learners of English as a foreign language has indicated that this apparent hierarchy of difficulty may explain, at least partly, some of the learners' errors in English.

Indeed, experiments have shown some quite surprising similarities in achievement between different groups of language learners, both first and foreign. Bailey, Madden and Krashen (1974), examining results from several experiments, show that both adults and children who are learning English as a second language perform very similarly to each other, although the adult level of performance was not so high as that of the children.

OVERGENERALISATION

Another approach to the explanation of learners' errors is that which H V George (1972), as well as other workers in the field, touches on. J Richards terms it 'overgeneralisation' and H V George 'redundancy reduction'. On the basis of his experience of the language, the learner constructs a deviant structure, for example.

a   We are visit the zoo.
b   She must goes.
c   Yesterday I walk to the shop and I buy . . .

As Richards points out, this type of error can be regarded as a blend of two structures in the 'standard version' of the language. The error might be made as a result of blending structures learnt early in the learning sequence. In the three sentences given as an example, sentence (a) shows a blending of the continuous and the simple present and in sentence (b) both the modal verb *and* the standard third person singular *-s* suffix are used. Sentence (c) is slightly different, in that the redundancy (the additional information which any natural language incorporates) is removed: the adverbial marker 'yesterday' is, for the learner, sufficient to indicate a time reference, and consequently the *-ed* is omitted from the stem of the verbs. In the first two examples, (a) and (b), the overgeneralisation is that of removing the necessity for concord, and overgeneralising the rule which states that in the present simple there are no suffixes except for the third person singular. In the case of (c) the redundancy involves the -*ed* form and 'yesterday', both indicating time past. The information in the message is, under optimum conditions, not interfered with − but with less favourable conditions, the listener would have only *one* indicator of 'time past' and could miss it, thus leading to failure to interpret the speaker's or writer's intention.

What actually gives rise to the overgeneralisation can be any one or more of a number of factors. Some possibilities are the manner or order in which the language items are presented by the teacher or the text; and the actual exercises which the learner is called upon to complete. For example, learners may produce the following incorrect responses:

exercise	**response**
She goes: (must)	She must goes.
I walk to the shop: (yesterday)	Yesterday I walk to the shop.

The general pedagogic dictum of 'never teach together what can be confused' is often a sound one. 'He sings' is often contrasted with 'he is singing' in the lessons and texts, after what seems like sufficient learning time. Soon after this the learner produces a blend of the two 'he is sings'.

INCOMPLETE APPLICATION OF RULES

In addition to overgeneralisation, most teachers will be familiar with the reverse side of the coin: incomplete application of rules. Richards suggests two possible causes here. One is the use of questions in the classroom, where the learner is encouraged to repeat the question or part of it in the answer, for example

Teacher   Do you read much?
Student   Yes, I read much.
or
Teacher   Ask her where she lives.
Student   Where you (she) live(s)?

The other possible cause is the fact that the learner may discover that he can communicate perfectly adequately using deviant forms.

MATERIAL-INDUCED ERRORS

Two further types of error which may be induced by teaching materials are (a) the 'false concept' and (b) ignorance of rule restrictions. An example of (a), which will be familiar to many teachers of English, is the use of the present continuous tense in the wrong situation. It is not uncommon in English teaching materials to see a series of pictures illustrating a sequence of actions, with the caption in the present continuous although the use of the tense in this context is unnatural. (See Figure 5.) A more appropriate context would be a radio commentary of a football match or a detective reporting over the phone the actions of a suspect, for example.

His alarm clock is ringing

He is getting up

He is washing

Figure 5

The problem with contrived use of language items is precisely that since they form data which the learner will use to form his hypotheses, the learner may be misled in his assumptions. Motivation, naturalness and a sensible context for the language are clearly vital, if we accept the view that learners will use the data presented to them actively, in order to test the use of the language items and form assumptions as to the kind of language they are learning.

It is probably even more difficult to avoid errors arising from ignorance of rule restriction than it is to avoid false conceptualisation. This is because such errors often involve the construction of false analogies, a very similar activity to what children do when experimenting with their own language. A learner, for example, may have cause to use the noun 'discussion', and recalls that it is linked to another noun or noun phrase with the preposition 'about' (eg 'a discussion about nuclear energy'). What then is more natural when the verb 'discuss' occurs, than to use it with the same preposition, leading to 'We discussed about the oil crisis'? Or, similarly, 'Tell him to write the letter' or 'Ask him to write the letter' may lead to 'Make him to write the letter'.

The suggestion made before — not to practise together things that can be confused — will not completely solve this problem; as we have seen, the learner is a far more active participant in the language-learning activity than we may have imagined. Once again it seems that errors are virtually inevitable.

ERROR AS A PART OF LANGUAGE CREATIVITY

Learners who are limited in their opportunities of listening to examples of the target language tend to form hypothetical rules about the new language on insufficient evidence. Learners need to create new utterances, but with limited experience of the target language, they may make mistakes.

This notice was seen in a hotel in China: 'A doctor is available for emergent visits'. The person who wrote the notice was aware of adjectival forms like 'urgent' versus the nominal form 'urgency', 'delinquent' versus 'delinquency'. He either knew the word 'emergency' or found it in the dictionary, marked as a noun. His limited English did not reach to 'noun plus noun' compounds to produce the correct form 'emergency visits'. He played safe, in one sense, and formed what would seem, on the face of it, an entirely regular form which should fit into the pattern: 'an' + adjective + 'visit'. It is, of course, in the nature of language to be unpredictable in certain places, and this happened to be one. The word 'emergent' exists, but it doesn't mean what the writer imagined it did. Nevertheless, the process leading to the error is clearly a creative one. (Selinker 1972 calls this an 'L_2 communication strategy'.) It is a natural activity of the human who interacts with his environment in the laudable attempt to make sense of it and to form it to his own ends.

This same creative activity led a student learning German to use the adjective *bissig* (which literally means 'liable to bite') in the wrong context. He had seen the adjective used in relation to dogs: *Achtung, bissiger Hund* ('Beware of the dog') so imagined he could use it to mean 'Beware of the teacher' and created the utterance *Achtung, bissiger Lehrer*! The teacher could easily have categorised the utterance as 'deviant' on the grounds of unusual collocation, but in fact his positive response had a great psychological effect on the student and his subsequent enthusiasm for learning German. This anecdote is intended to illustrate the fact that one of the main causes of error, though not the only one, is precisely that creativity and adventurousness in students that the alert and responsive teacher at any level will wish to encourage.

It should be made clear at this stage that there are at least two types of creativity in language use. The first type, which is being referred to here, is the ability in the learner to use the parts of the language that he has learnt in order to say something that he may not have heard before; it is precisely the same process which leads the mother tongue child to produce the form 'goed'. The learner is drawing certain conclusions about how the language behaves, using as evidence what he has seen of the target language. It is this type of behaviour that teachers would surely wish to encourage among language learners, despite the fact that it may, on occasion, lead to 'deviant' language forms. The problem is that when exams are being prepared for, both teachers and taught expect a rather more defensive mode of behaviour; it is often thought that it is considerably safer, in an exam which sets out to assess a learner's control of the language code, to say what can be said safely rather than take risks.

The second type of creativity is that which is more usually covered by the term 'creative arts'. It is quite rare for people to be able to create works of literature in a language other than their own, even if it has been as thoroughly learnt as their mother tongue. Joseph Conrad, whose first language was Polish, but wrote novels in English, and Samuel Beckett who is Irish but writes in French, are clearly *not* the norm among writers.

3.3 Foreign and second language learning

Interference from another language has already been mentioned as one of the possible sources of error in language learning. Let us now look at the different forms this may take for the learner of English as a foreign language and the learner of English as a second language. One hears the target language in a classroom, where his only chance to practise the language occurs. The other lives in a different type of environment where he can see English in use around him, on advertising hoardings for example, and hear it used by his fellow countrymen in certain situations in his society.

FOREIGN LANGUAGE ERRORS
Let us consider first of all the learner who hears his English mainly in the classroom; in other words, the learner of English as a 'foreign language'. The errors he makes will relate closely to his own

formation of an 'interlanguage' (see page 11 and the Glossary). They may also arise as a result of the data he is presented with by the textbook, or by the teacher, who may, for example, consistently 'mispronounce' a given sound, or constantly make a grammatical error. We would of course hope not to find actual grammatical errors made by teachers or in textbooks, but it is possible that a manner or order of presentation may lead to the formation by the learner of certain ideas or 'hypotheses' which may not accord with the actual facts of the target language. For example, some textbooks introduce the present continuous tense at a very early stage. This tends to happen because it seems to be the easiest tense to demonstrate in the classroom, and one of the most 'productive' tenses in so far as it can be used to teach further items of the language. As we mentioned on page 33, the order in which items are presented and the exercises on them may cause overgeneralisation or confusion. This is difficult to prove, but given what research shows us about language learning and the usual order of introducing language items in textbooks, this explanation at least seems plausible. The point being underlined here is that the error in the foreign language situation really has to be a result of something that happens in the classroom, since it is usually only here that the learner comes into contact with the target language.

SECOND LANGUAGE ERRORS

This, however, is not the case when we consider the learner of English in an environment where the language is in regular use outside the classroom. We assume that the target language inside the classroom, the language of the textbook and the target of the teacher is one of the standard varieties of English, British, American, Australian, etc. In very many countries where English is used as an official language, and perhaps as a *lingua franca* (that is, a language of communication for those with no common local language), the varieties of English heard outside the classroom may be very different from the standard variety which is the target *inside*. An example of a country where this is the case is Ghana, with over fifty languages for a population of approximately nine million. It is not surprising that, in this situation, English outside the classroom in Ghana develops some special characteristics of both pronunciation and structure. These features which are not found in any of the standard varieties of English could be termed both 'errors' and 'mistakes'. But, given that the language functions efficiently as a medium of communication, would we be entirely justified in talking about 'errors'? As with American English, so Ghanaian English differs in both lexical and structural items from British English, since there are, naturally, concepts and objects not found in Britain or British English.

For example:

guarantee shoes Platform-soled shoes, originally sold with a guarantee of quality.

chopbar A type of open-air snackbar serving hot food.

Firestone tyre pass tyre A very common advertisement, using 'pass' for the comparative and meaning both 'passes' and 'is better than' other tyres.

The car will pick you at the airport Pick you up.

In this type of environment there is much more difficulty in judging error. However, if a teacher believes that language is not taught only to pass exams, more variations become acceptable. If we talk of 'Ghanaian English', we are simplifying the issue. There are, as with any regional variety of a language, many different levels and types of Ghanaian English. The language used by a lecturer talking to his colleagues in a university seminar will differ from that used by the same lecturer when addressing a policeman or perhaps a market trader, on the limited occasions when he uses English in these situations. Furthermore, the English used by one policeman to another would again be different. It is an over-simplification to regard the non-standard utterances as 'wrong'. We need different criteria. Perhaps something along these lines might suffice: does the addressee understand the speaker's meaning quickly and clearly? This is clearly a major topic. It raises the whole issue of what we mean by 'correctness' in language. (See Figure 6.) This is discussed further in the next chapter.

A problem occurs when a listener new to the environment appears, or when a speaker accustomed to one perhaps rather limited variety of local English moves into a different setting, needing the language for different purposes. It is of interest that these problems also occur among first language speakers. This was noted in 1972 by Doughty, Pearce and Thornton who attributed the silence of some students in a new environment to their lack of familiarity with suitable language.

As far as the classroom teacher is concerned, what causes deviations in the case of second language learning is precisely the fact that the target language is being used outside the classroom for communication purposes, and it is natural for the effects of this to carry over into the school. Indeed, it would seem to be potentially counter-productive to treat these commonly used forms as 'incorrect' in any way, since they are everyday currency in the 'real world' beyond the school walls. On the other hand, the teacher clearly cannot encourage the use of this type of local spoken English in, say, the writing of pieces of formal work. What seems necessary here is an approach which stresses the relationship of different types of language to different situations. It may be asking something new of many teachers to admit that in language, as in many other fields of human experience, there may be no such thing as correct and incorrect answers to every question, but rather, more or less appropriate ones.

In more practical terms, what can the teacher actually do? One way of dealing with this problem might be to gather examples of as many different types of English used in the country as possible — perhaps this could be treated as a class or school project. Different media using English for the transmission of information should be included: advertisements (both written and, where possible, spoken on radio and film), English used in newspapers, on labels and

An example of a 'Ghanaian English' poem, from a book written and published in Ghana. The poems are suggested by 'mottoes' on the buses. (p. 71, No Time to Die, K.G.Kyei and H.Schreckenbach, 1975)

I NO BE LIKE YOU

I no be like you,
    at all; what!
Proper libilibi* man like you.
Today you go speak so for here,
Tomorrow you go talk different
    for there.
Then because of you
    big trouble come for
    between people plenty like that.
I no be like you,
    at all; what!

                    Wife-chaser like you,
                    Boast-man like you
                    You want everything here
                        for Ghana for yourself alone.
                    You chop*
                    You don't want your brother too
                        for chop some self.
                    Selfish man like you.
                    I no be like you,
                        at all; what!

Teef man, Burglar man like you,
You you hide corner corner for dark time
    and teef* woman shoes
    teef shirts
    teef Charlie-wote* sandals
People worka worka hard buy am
From broken-time* money.

                    I no be like you,
                        at all; what!
                    You you take your big mouth
                    Like chimpanzee bottom
                    For talk foolish foolish talk
                        for people back.
                    I no be like you,
                        at all; what!

libilibi crooked, devious   **Charlie-wote** rubber sandals
chop eat   **broken-time** overtime   **teef** steal (from 'thief')

Figure 6

packaging on manufactured products, in news broadcasts and on television, in business and other communications. It is important for the class to collect as wide a set of examples as possible, both in writing and, if possible, on tape. If English is used as a *lingua franca*, as, say, the language or one of the languages of the playground, then this too would be useful material.

The next stage after collecting examples of 'local varieties of English' would be some kind of study of the differences and similarities. The depth and sophistication of this stage would obviously depend largely both on the age of the students and the formal grammatical knowledge of the teacher. One interesting approach to this type of problem has already been made. Jean Ure's *Bridge Course* (1974) follows a method close to that outlined here and also includes some study of local languages and their use in different situations. This overtly more advanced work was designed for teacher training level, and was written in Ghana.

A further extension of this work is to play to students recordings of examples of various British accents (Scottish, Cockney, Geordie, etc), and to show examples of different styles of written language in Britain. This is evidence from another source of the variation in language in general and in English in particular. There could be no firm conclusion emerging from this work as to 'correct' and 'incorrect' forms. The aim would be to encourage a more sensitive attitude to the relationship between the types of language and the environments in which they are used.

Summary

An attempt has been made to describe at least some of the many possible causes of language learners' errors.

1 Carelessness, which is not always the student's fault.
2 Interference from the learner's first language is now believed to play a smaller — but still significant — part in causing errors.

3   Translation from the first language can lead to difficulty where there are not exact parallels between the two languages. And what, in any case, *is* an 'exact parallel'?

4   Contrastive analysis can indicate some areas of difficulty but is of limited use because of the problem of analysing the languages in sufficient detail and finding a framework for comparison.

5   Even native speakers seem to learn their language according to an order of difficulty.

6   Both native speakers learning their mother tongue and foreign learners tend to make errors by applying what they already know of the language to a new situation where the same rules do not apply.

7   The learner may be able to make himself understood by only applying some of the rules and continue to produce deviant forms.

8   The learner may not interpret the material presented to him in the way intended by the teacher or textbook writer.

9   False analogies may be made due to ignorance of rule restrictions.

10 Language can be unpredictable and the learner may make errors by using the language he has already learnt to say or write something he has not ever heard or read.

While the causes of errors made by learners of a foreign language may be limited to their exposure to the target language in the classroom, learners of a second language are also influenced by the varieties of that language that they come into contact with outside the classroom.

It may appear on reading this chapter that it is a wonder that learners ever manage to produce error-free forms. Luckily for teachers, they do!

4 Errors and mistakes in listening and speaking

There was enough evidence in Chapter 3 to make teachers think it is a wonder that language learners ever actually manage to produce linguistically acceptable forms. In this chapter we will look at errors or mistakes made in speech. Teachers may then be surprised that listeners can *understand* everyday unscripted speech!

In considering errors and mistakes in listening and speaking, suggestions will be made for remedial teaching. It will become apparent that there is nothing different about remedial teaching from any other 'good teaching practice'. The important points are that the method adopted for remedial teaching should allow the learner to approach the problem in a different way and not in the way that caused difficulties first time round; secondly, the teacher should avoid making the learner feel that the need for the remedial exercise is his fault.

4.1 Native speaker slips

It must be fairly clear to most language teachers that in natural, unscripted speech there are likely to be more of the mistake and lapse types of deviation from an ideal than in writing, unless the writing is the result of work at great speed with little or no time for correction. When we speak, even in our own language, we sometimes make mistakes; these are often so minor, and indeed, so common that the listener is not even aware of them. One such mistake is to transpose sounds accidentally. This mistake is called a Spoonerism after the

Oxford lecturer who constantly changed initial consonants around. This is just one example:

'I saw you fight a liar in the back quad; in fact, you have tasted the whole worm.'

Because listeners are generally paying attention to the content rather than to the form in which it is expressed, many people are unaware of the actual nature of spoken language. Speakers are engaged in a highly complex activity. To many people it is not immediately apparent, but a great deal of planning is involved. The speaker's attention is divided equally between content and the problems of formulating the message and unless the speaker has had extensive experience of 'thinking on his feet', the activities will interfere with each other.

If a learner of a language has his attention drawn to a slip he has made, such as using singular verb with a plural subject, he will probably find it hard to believe that an L_1 speaker can make the same kind of mistake. But in fact most speech emerges in fits and starts, often aided by gestures and bearing little resemblance to the ideal 'grammar book' version of the language. We may feel that speaking a language fluently means speaking with no hesitations but this is rarely true even of the native speaker. It is usually only practised public speakers and those speaking from scripts, such as television presenters, who speak fluently with no hesitations or mistakes.

Many native speakers would be unaware of the way they speak unless they heard a recording of themselves. The following is a transcription of a tape-recording of the author speaking in a seminar in West Africa. It is a fairly typical example of 'educated' speech in which the message and the form it takes is being 'planned' as the speaker goes along.

'This is er an an interesting thing because this obviously comes to one of the fundamental issues er er that I mentioned in the introduction and that is the model of prob... er, the problem of model in well, er, obviously what we're concerned with is the West African Exams Council area, for English.'

The normal places for pauses or corrections are, firstly, at the beginnings and ends of 'sentences'. ('Sentence' is in quotation marks because it is a *written*, not a spoken, convention.) This is the usual place for speakers to breathe and plan ahead. Secondly, pauses and corrections occur at the ends of phrases while the following part of the 'skeleton sentence' is planned, the next noun phrase, prepositional phrase, verb or adverbial phrase. This pause is frequently 'filled' by characteristic noises like 'em', 'er', 'well', etc. Thirdly, there is often a hesitation before the first content word: after the planning of the structure of the phrase, the precise words to be used need to be considered − for example, 'a − a disgusting spectacle' or 'a − disgusting spectacle'.

There are some English language textbooks on the market which incorporate exercises involving the editing of excerpts of genuine speech forms, transcribed from tape-recordings, into the usual written form. There is an example of this type of work, from Cook, V J (1974) *English Topics*, Oxford University Press, pp 67, 68.

Unedited Transcript

DARRYL WHITELEY: I think takeaways is all part of this er lack of sociability that's increasing all the time. Like pubs. At one time you you you would expect to go into a pub where you didn't know anybody and you'd expect there was a fair chance of getting into conversation with somebody there. Now they're all being done up and therefore places to go already for people in closed groups: they don't mix with the other groups there, they just go in their group. I suppose you go to a restaurant, you could go to a restaurant and start talking to people perhaps although less so, whereas now takeaway you just go in, get your food, and take it back into your ready-made group and and eat and talk with the people in that group.

PETER BURCH: I think this is typical of our society, isn't it? We we tend to avoid people rather than to to seek out company; we we prefer to withdraw and sit...

PAM COOK: Yes, because I mean how often does one go to a restaurant in a big group like the Chinese do? I mean the Chinese when they go out they take everyone from the smallest child — aunts, uncles, the lot. It's a wonderful occasion. But I mean you know you don't see this very often. You do have sort of um the grand occasion where you're all got the carnations laid out on the table and speeches and everything but I mean you know just...

PETER BURCH: Very rare.

PAM COOK: Very rare. No, I mean this does happen as a social occasion, Peter.

PETER BURCH: Births, marriages and deaths.

PAM COOK: Yes, but how often does it happen as a just a whole lot of people together go go out and have a meal? Not very often.

DARRYL WHITELEY: Very rarely.

Edited Transcript

DARRYL WHITELEY: I think takeaway restaurants are part of the lack of sociability that's increasing all the time. Take pubs for instance. At one time you could go into a pub where you didn't know anybody and you'd expect to get into conversation with somebody there. Now they're places to go to in a group; people don't mix with the other groups there, they just go in their group. Similarly in takeaway restaurants you go in, get your food and take it away without going outside your own group.

PETER BURCH: I think this is typical of our society, isn't it? We tend to avoid people rather than seek them out.

PAM COOK: I agree. How often do people go to a restaurant in a big group like the Chinese do? When the Chinese go out they take everyone from the smallest child. It's a wonderful occasion. Here you don't see this very often except for the grand occasion when you've got speeches and everything.

PETER BURCH: And they're very rare.

PAM COOK: Yes, but they do happen.

PETER BURCH: Only for births, marriages, and deaths.

PAM COOK: But how often do people go out to have a meal together as a group?
DARRY WHITELEY: Very rarely.

This kind of exercise is probably as useful to the teacher of English as it is to the learner, since it enables him to see the typical 'ungrammaticality' of normal speech.

4.2 Language learner slips

So much for the usual hesitations of a first language speaker; now for our language learner: how would his hesitations compare with these characteristics we have noted? Learners, when speaking a language new to them, frequently feel that their speech should be free of hesitation. Since this is not true in their first language, it is hardly likely that they will be able to produce hesitation-free utterances when talking without preparation in a language which is less familiar to them. This attitude may well be influenced by the type of oral tasks which many learners undertake in the classroom, where, traditionally, great importance is attached to economy of time and correctness. Thus hesitations are not encouraged and the 'right answer' is the target, generally as the result of either a written or spoken 'cue' from a text or the teacher. Often there is no opportunity to express one's own thoughts and feelings in the classroom. In a drill exercise, where students are expected to answer quickly, there is little likelihood of hesitations occurring. This type of experience may lead both teacher and learner to the conclusion that hesitation is in some sense undesirable.

The learner has at his disposal much less of the language than his native speaker counterpart, so the planning activities will be concerned with fewer alternatives. On the other hand, there is a very important extra level of planning to be undertaken — that of consciously recalling language items and the patterns in which they occur. Often in class the student performs only this latter type of planning; the content of his utterances is controlled because he is required to perform certain actions on data presented to him in the form of exercises, blanks to be filled, or puzzles to be solved.

It is relatively easy for teachers to deceive themselves into thinking that students have achieved fluency in the target language when they can do the exercises in their books quickly and well. However, as we have seen, the process of using a language to express one's own ideas (which must surely be the aim, in part at least, of any oral course) involves much more planning. The fluent speaker — even of his own language — is not necessarily a speaker who speaks without hesitations. Stumblings in the middle of phrases, even of words, or attempting to get the right inflexional ending on a verb *is* characteristic of the second language speaker.

A useful teaching technique might be to teach older, more sophisticated learners *where* to hesitate, and also some of the sounds made by native speakers when pausing. Since the place of hesitation is more important than the sound made, non-native teachers should not worry too much about the sounds. But an exercise on the positions of hesitations might look like this:

1 You are not certain about the underlined words in the following sentences. Make a suitable 'pause noise' before the words in the place indicated by the dots.
a . . . I have never seen such a tall man before.
b They visited us only . . . two weeks ago last Friday.
c I could have told him the news . . . if only I had been able to see him before he left.

At a later stage the teacher could provide a model of natural speech, with hesitations, for the students to adapt. For example:

Teacher   I was born in (place) and went to school in (place) when I was (ten) years old. My favourite subjects were (History), (English) and (Art). I think that if I hadn't become a teacher, I'd have been a . . . etc.

The students then produce similar utterances about themselves, with pauses in the appropriate places.

As they become more competent in the target language, it is important that learners should continue this type of work, but in a less controlled form. The kind of exercise which would be of most use is that which gives students a reason to talk to each other, to share information which is necessary in order to achieve some goal. Two excellent examples of books where this style of work is developed are Maley and Duff (1978) and Sturtridge and Geddes (1978).

4.3 Should we allow students to be human?

Should English language teachers expect students to be able to produce a type of 'ideal model' sentence, when native speakers do not do this themselves? Vivian Cook (1979) asks whether we demand standards of our students that even native speakers could not maintain. But, very often, the model of spoken English on tapes which accompany textbooks are scripted dialogues, read by trained actors. This can give both student and teacher a very false idea of what is the actual norm for unscripted speech. By giving the learner a target which is not realistic, we are encouraging him not to risk making an utterance if he feels unsure of how to say it before he opens his mouth. This will produce the usual reaction of the English language class when an English visitor appears. The class is asked by the teacher to ask the visitor questions or to talk to him. This is usually followed by a deafening silence. There are two major reasons for this: one is that it is extremely difficult to 'ask questions' of someone without knowing anything about them and the other (which is more important) is that learners tend to feel that the entire question must be formulated before they begin to speak.

Learners need to be given the confidence to begin a question without planning it out in advance. They need to be encouraged to reformulate what they want to say as they go along, just as a native speaker does. This will only be discouraged if the teacher penalises or comments unfavourably on hesitations. The same applies to minor errors in grammar. Providing the meaning is clear, it may well not be worth correcting them. After all, native speakers make grammatical mistakes themselves. There is linguistic evidence that there may be such things as ungrammatical sentences spoken between L_1 speakers which are nevertheless acceptable to many mother tongue speakers; for example, in spoken language this utterance would probably be accepted by a large number of listeners: 'Chinese food is the kind of food which two hours after a meal you feel as if you haven't eaten it' (Smith and Wilson 1979).

CORRECTING EXERCISES IN FLUENCY

Fluency involves the ability to be imprecise and to 'talk around' a subject, using expressions like 'sort of', 'kind of', with the name of an object which approximates to the actual word. For example, 'a kind of statue to help us remember people' − a memorial, 'a kind of boat for carrying people short distances' − a ferry, and so on. Naturally, when there are too many errors or mistakes, the meaning can become obscured. But if the teacher does hear errors which worry him, the course of action to take is not necessarily to correct the error immediately but note those which he feels need dealing with and come back to them on another occasion. The points which the teacher may wish to make a brief note of would be those teaching points which seem generally to be causing problems. For example, if, in a class of beginners, the teacher hears repeatedly the form 'How many windows your house got?' while the learners are trying to find their 'partner' with the same type of house on their picture, then the question form may need to be re-taught.

Here is a suggested method for noting down the mistakes that you feel are important. First draw up a list of language points that an activity is likely to produce: tenses, prepositions, adjective order, particular points of pronunciation etc. Then, while listening to the students performing the activity, simply place a tick against the particular class of mistake or error. It would be a good idea to leave some spaces vacant so that further remarks can be made. But in general it is advisable to keep writing to a minimum for two reasons: first, it saves time and enables you to listen and second, it will appear less obvious to students. This method applies particularly to activities and language games (see in the same series Revell 1979 and Rixon 1981). In such cases, it is inappropriate to draw attention to the medium of communication, since the point of the activity is to encourage a less self-conscious use of the language and to approach as closely as possible in a classroom environment a 'natural' use of the language.

It should be understood here that it is quite often a *build-up* of errors that blocks communication. If the number of possible meanings rises above a certain number, then the listener has to carry too many options in his head, and difficulty arises in sorting out the speaker's intentions. The advantage for the learner himself in the situation of a game or role-play is that he himself will be able to judge whether or not his meaning has been understood. If not, he can try to express it again. For example, if the speaker is trying to describe a picture that he can see in such a way that the listener can draw it, then he will very quickly be able to determine whether his meaning is clear. If the listener draws what the speaker thinks he has described, then all is well. If not, some re-phrasing is necessary.

Many teachers are likely to have severe doubts about not stopping a learner in order to correct errors in speech as soon as they occur, since, runs the usual argument, if the learner makes mistakes, surely these are the forms both he and his colleagues learn. As we have seen earlier, however, (see Chapter 2) this is not necessarily the case. The view which is being put forward here is that fluency in speech can only come about through the opportunity to use the language while not having to worry unduly over the form in which the message is transmitted; in other words, it can only come about when students feel sufficiently confident in, firstly, their ability to use the language they are learning for exchanging information and, secondly, their teacher's wish to stand aside and allow them to find their own way. This stage of confidence is necessarily founded on a great deal of careful work which leads up to the point at which students can be left to their own devices. This preparation will include careful teaching of grammatical structures (whether or not the teacher is primarily concerned with a 'functional approach') and vocabulary and pronunciation.

PRONUNCIATION

This book will not deal at length with teaching pronunciation. This is an area which merits a book in its own right, such as *Pronunciation Skills* by Paul Tench in this series. Some important points will, however, be introduced at this stage.

Many teachers will at times have despaired of ever teaching their classes certain sounds. The sounds which cause most difficulty are generally those which do not exist in the mother tongue and are confused with or substituted by sounds in the mother tongue which seem similar. After concentrated practice the students are successful in producing the sound. But then, when later the same sound occurs in an exercise or a word is used featuring the sound in a freer type of activity, the sound once again 'reverts' to its former state. As soon as the students' concentration on the sound itself is relaxed, regression tends to take place, especially when the attention is focused on another aspect of the message other than its pronunciation. This is especially true of older students, and it is generally believed nowadays that while it is quite possible theoretically for learners over the age of puberty to master a grammatical system efficiently, it gets increasingly difficult for them to overcome the barrier of the sound system, the phonology. Younger learners, on the other hand, can frequently become indistinguishable from native speakers.

The important term to note here, however, is the word 'system'; that is, a range of choices where the selection of one option necessarily rules out the others. The more usual outcome of language learning after puberty is a failure to master the entire system, but to progress up to a point at which successful communication can take place. At this point 'fossilisation' (a point at which development towards the target language norm stops) often occurs unless the learner remains conscious of 'difficult' sounds. There are examples of this among immigrant communities around the world, where despite relatively long stays in the new country, the pronunciation of many individuals remains imperfect by mother tongue standards. The teacher, when faced with fossilisation, needs to answer the question, 'Can this learner be understood with relative ease by most users of the target language with whom he is likely to come into contact?'

'Pedagogical Norms'

It is not always easy to know what aims are appropriate for all language learners. A child learning a foreign language at school may never have the chance to converse with a user of that target language or he may later need the language for business meetings, travelling abroad or study purposes. In the case of a learner in a second language environment, he will need the language, perhaps, in the early stages for use with his fellow-countrymen with whom he may have no local language in common. The pronunciation needed, even expected, in this situation would differ from that needed by a businessman about to undertake a tour of another country where English is spoken as a first language; in which case the most appropriate model would be the pronunciation of the country concerned.

In considering the question of teaching pronunciation, Albert Valdman (1975) has recommended what he calls 'pedagogical norms'; these are sounds which may belong to a dialect of the target language, but not, perhaps, to the standard. They are not likely to be misunderstood by the mother tongue listener. An example in English: let us consider the sound /ʌ/ as in 'cup'. There is a group of sounds in this area which provide problems for speakers of other languages because of the apparent closeness of the sounds to each other. For speakers of many languages, the distinction between 'cup' /kʌp/ and 'cap' /kæp/ is barely discernible and so errors are made. One way around this problem may be to teach a sound closer to the northern English sound in the same word — resembling the southern English sound in 'book'. The /æ/ sound ('cap') could be given a quality more like /ɛ/ in order to differentiate it.

A disadvantage of this is that the students will not hear these forms from other native speakers: this is true, but we are here discussing production of the sounds, not their comprehension. Under normal conditions of language use, the context will make it quite clear whether the word being referred to is, in this instance, 'cup' or 'cap'; problems of comprehension of speech (apart from a pronunciation test featuring isolated words, or words in carefully concocted contexts such as 'Did you see a ship/sheep?') are generally not related to the failure to recognise these sound distinctions. But learners can receive messages accurately sooner than they can transmit them, so the fact that there might be a discrepancy between the learner's speech sounds and the native speaker's need not lead to a learner's failure to comprehend a native speaker's spoken message. It has been ascertained (Ladefoged 1967) that even first language speakers vary considerably in the quality they give to vowels but they have a clearly demarcated system which the listener, after a short period of assessment, can interpret without difficulty. The learner's sounds are not stable, nor are they in a constant relationship to each other; this is why it is necessary to enable them to develop a system, rather than to work at isolated sounds.

Intonation and stress

Much more important than vowel sounds are consonants, and more important than either of these 'segmental' aspects of spoken language is intonation and stress (the 'suprasegmentals'). Experiments filtering out vowel qualities have shown that the message is still clear enough to be understood. But when consonants disappear, the message can barely be interpreted. Intonation patterns (the 'tunes' of pronunciation) are notoriously difficult to describe, even more so to teach. It appears that when native speakers misunderstand learners of their language, the most frequent cause is that the learner's mother tongue 'tunes' arouse unexpected reactions. For example, an Englishman might misinterpret an Italian intonation as conveying extreme excitement when in fact the Italian is speaking English with what would be a normal statement pattern in his own language. The transfer of intonation patterns from the mother tongue to the target language can produce unintentional overtones of meaning.

An interesting piece of practical advice is given by Stevick (1976), who suggests that English students learning another language should attempt to imitate native speakers of that target language speaking English. Thus, an Englishman who can 'do a French accent' might well be able to carry over the sounds which seem to him to characterise the Frenchman speaking English into his French pronunciation. Chapters 4 and 5 of Paul Tench's book in this series are particularly valuable on the teaching of rhythm, intonation and stress.

Syllable and stress timing

One point of pronunciation which can lead to a breakdown in communication is the changing of stress patterns. English is a 'stress-timed' language (see page 130). This means, briefly, that the main stresses in an utterance will fall at approximately regular intervals, no matter how many 'weak' syllables intervene. It is this phenomenon which causes speakers of other languages to comment on the English speaker's 'slurred' speech. In individual words, too, there is a characteristic main stress. If either of these features (normal sentence stress or normal word stress) are changed, then comprehension is immediately interfered with. The typical 'machine gun' sound of the Frenchman (whose language has a roughly equal amount of time on each syllable) or the West African is difficult for the native English speaker to understand until he has had the opportunity to become accustomed to the sound. Similarly, it is difficult for the speaker of the 'syllable-timed' language to understand normal English pronunciation. One point to emerge from this is that it is important for students of English to hear (on tape or on the radio or live, when possible) examples of normal everyday speech in addition to the carefully produced and modulated tones of the actor on tapes specially produced for language teaching.

Another way of overcoming this problem of teaching stress patterns is by using the 'limerick', the comic verse form which relies for much of its effect on the strongly marked rhythm. Teachers could demonstrate and encourage students to read aloud some of these verses. Consider the following well known example:

> There 'was a young 'lady of 'Niger
> Who 'smiled as she 'rode on a 'tiger.
> They re'turned from the 'ride
> With the 'lady in'side
> And the 'smile on the 'face of the 'tiger.

As can be seen, the rhythmic pattern involves three stressed syllables each in the first and second lines, two in the next two lines and three once again in the final, fifth line. When recited, it is important that the stresses come at regular intervals. The number of unstressed syllables between the stresses need not make much difference to this, since in English they can be hurried over at a greater pace. Compare line 1 with line 5 of the limerick.

Line 1 begins: There was . . .
Line 5 begins: And the smile . . .

In line 5, the two weak syllables 'And the . . .' would normally be said in the same length of time as the one weak (unstressed) syllable in line 1, 'There . . .' The time given to each of the weak syllables in the final line will be about half that given to 'There' in the first line. This is a very flexible system. Consider the following:

> A ' very old ' man of Ja'pan

and

       An in'credibly old ' man of Ja'pan

The second of these two alternative opening lines for another limerick would take the same time to read as the first, despite the far greater number of weak syllables. However, this can only be true up to a point.

       A ' very old ' man of Ja'pan
       Wrote ' verses that ' no-one could ' scan.
       When ' asked why this ' was,
       He re'plied, 'It's be'cause
       I ' always try to get as many ' words into the last line
       as I possibly ' can.

The final line is fully intended to destroy the rhythmic effect, as part of the humour. 'Scan' here means roughly 'to work out the rhythmic pattern of a poem'.

As we have seen, the stress-timing of the limerick is also a characteristic of English speech. This is what makes it a useful teaching tool. It is worth re-emphasising here a point made at the beginning of the chapter: such a teaching technique can be used as successfully for initial teaching of stress as for remedial teaching to eradicate errors. 'Good practice' in general teaching is 'good practice' in remedial situations.

THE LISTENER'S ROLE

A final point that needs to be made is that the process of comprehension of spoken language is normally a matter of constant negotiation between speaker and listener. This is certainly true between mother tongue speakers, and it is even more so when either the speaker or listener or both are second or foreign language speakers. Both the listener and the speaker in any dialogue need to be actively making sense of the sounds. In a conversation between two native speakers probably neither will notice any errors that are made because not every feature of speech is essential for the message to be clear. However, if the speaker is a learner of the language, he may make mistakes that the listener has to allow for in order to understand the message. If the listener is not a native speaker then his role is harder because he may simply not understand some of the words said to him; he cannot then afford to miss any other carriers of meaning (as the native speaker can) if he is to understand the gist of what is said to him.

As far as the classroom teacher is concerned, he needs to encourage in his students a participatory role in language activities. Students should be motivated to speak and to listen in the classroom. It is obviously difficult to encourage a naturally quiet, shy personality to enjoy free communication but there are a number of activities that can help stimulate the desire to participate in sharing information and opinions. By using activities in the classroom, the teacher can go a long way towards demonstrating that errors in speech do not immediately result in a breakdown in communication. Students can discover that there is enjoyment in using another language successfully and that success can be measured not in the number of corrections to be remembered but in whether or not there has been an exchange of information.

The type of activity suggested is one which involves sharing information for a particular purpose − for example, a project to discover the ways of processing a local product, say, coffee or cocoa, together with its marketing procedures. Groups of students can find out information under a variety of headings and, on returning to the classroom, share with others the information they have, so that the entire group finally has a more or less complete picture. Students at a lower level can take part in 'jigsaw' listening activities. The learners in groups listen to one of three or four different versions of a particular event and discuss what they have heard. Then one member of each group gets together in a new group and they all share the information they have got from the different versions they listened to, in order to reach some kind of complete account. An example of this type of activity is given here, but see also Sturtridge and Geddes 1978.

Listening exercise

Each speaker is given a typed sheet of notes. They study the notes then record their respective versions of the accident. This stage of the exercise is better done by the teacher(s) and some colleagues, or by L₁ English speakers, unless the class is made up of very advanced students. The class is divided into three groups and each group listens to *one* of the recordings. Groups then disperse and compare stories to try and find out the truth. Finally, groups come together in the classroom and compare notes about their ideas. The fourth version, the eyewitness, is then played and groups discover how close they were to the truth.

Notes for red car driver (male)

Driving slowly down Market Street to an appointment, about half past three, on 12th June. That damn green car — never did trust women drivers.

They never look where they're going.

Street too narrow for modern traffic — these old towns are very dangerous.

Coming down the street at a perfectly reasonable speed,
this wretched kid runs out into the road, I had to turn the wheel to miss it.

Mothers should keep their kids under control.

That green car, going all over the road, on MY side of the road.

Clearly HER fault.

She was trying to overtake, pass the bus, all those children in the back of her car, I'm not surprised she wasn't looking. She shot out from behind the bus very fast indeed, and I couldn't possibly miss her.

Yes, my car's an MG — a red one.

Notes for green car driver (female)

It was the 12th June at about 3.45.

Driving along Market Street in my car, a green Ford Cortina.

Driving slowly, as I'd only just turned into the street from the school.

Also, following a bus — moving slowly too. The bus seemed to stop and go over to the left.

I turned my wheel to the right, to see what was in front of the bus to pass him very carefully, the street is narrow, and I always drive slowly there along that part of the road. Then that red car drove straight into me, making such a loud noise, he must have been going very fast. He was trying to stop.

But he didn't stop soon enough, and he hit me.

Notes for bus driver (male)

Driving down Market street — I do it every two hours these days.

Every day of the week, too, so I know it pretty well.

Suddenly saw this little boy with his mum — just come from school, I expect — it was about 3.40 or so, the bus was on time, I remember that.

Well, this little kid, he runs out into the road.

His ball had fallen out of his bag, and he ran after it. There was this red car coming down Market Street VERY fast — too fast.

Thought he was going to hit the kid, but he swerved to the right.

I was moving slowly — just pulled away from a bus stop by the Town Hall.

Turned my wheel to the left and stopped. I saw this green car in my mirror — driver seemed to be talking to someone. She was going slowly behind me and she tried to pull over slowly to her right and pass me.

Red car going much too fast, couldn't stop, she didn't see him in time.

The little boy was lucky he wasn't hurt. But drivers do need to be careful in that narrow bit of road.

Notes for spectator/eyewitness (either male or female)

Oh yes, I saw it all happen — that was last Wednesday, the, erm, 12th. Yes.

Always walk along Market Street at that time, about twenty to four, lived here all my life, know everyone, like to say hello to the shopkeepers — they're all my friends, I know everyone in this town.

Yes, that red car that came down the street — Mr Jones — he's always in a hurry, he is. Late for a meeting, I expect.

And the lady in the green car — Mrs Smith — oh, a nice lady she is, always has time to speak to people. Very kind too.

She always picks up her friends' children from the school near there.

Had them with her in the car, she did. Lucky no-one was hurt, is what I say. She never drives fast, 'cos she's nearly always got these kids in the back. And as for that little boy that ran out into the road and started it all, he should be told not to do it again — he might be badly hurt — or someone else might.

Summary

1 Even speakers using their own language virtually inevitably make some mistakes or lapses in normal rapid, unscripted speech. This is because speakers are occupied in thinking ahead about the content of what they want to say while they are actually speaking. Hesitations, both silent and sounded, are an almost essential part of normal speech. Indeed if people spoke in the style of written language they would soon find that listeners had difficulty understanding them as it is an essential feature of the spoken language to incorporate redundancy in order to lighten the burden of comprehension.

2 Learners should be taught the sounds to make which show that the speaker has not yet finished and where to pause. Fluency should be seen not simply in the light of producing grammatically perfect sentences but of saying what the speaker wishes to say while forming the utterance as he goes along.

3 Where pronunciation problems are concerned, it is not always necessary to teach only those sounds produced by a speaker of the standard form of the target language. It is only important that the sounds taught should be sufficiently differentiated from each other not to cause confusion. Learners need to hear as wide a variety as possible of different native speakers' voices and accents.

4 Vowel sounds are not as important in speech as consonants, and these are not so vital as intonation and stress.

5 It is not only the task of the speaker to make himself understood, but also that of the listener to make some effort to understand. This process of negotiation is a common feature of speech between native speakers and it becomes even more necessary when a speaker or listener is not using his own language. Students need practice in order to gain confidence to undertake this form of negotiation. The teacher's attitude to the learner's errors and manner of treating them during this time is of crucial importance.

5 Errors and mistakes in writing

5.1 Writing as a secondary skill

While listening and speaking are usually regarded as 'primary' language skills, reading and writing are frequently referred to as 'secondary'. These terms do not reflect any attitude as to their relative importance in societies where increasing value is being placed on the skills of literacy. The terms refer rather to the usual order of learning them. People learn to speak their mother tongue before they learn to write it and in some cases the primary skills are the only language skills acquired. It has been demonstrated by many scientists (for example, Lenneberg 1967) that even severely mentally handicapped humans can operate with the *spoken* language. There are still languages spoken in some parts of the world which have no written form and whose speakers, if they have the opportunity to become literate, must do so in a language other than their own. There seems also to be a widespread feeling that writing is, in some way, more difficult than speaking. It is the language skill with which the native speaker has most problems, and one which is not mastered at all by some of them. Why should this be so? What are the features of writing which make it harder, and thus more susceptible to error?

5.2 Characteristics of written information

In attempting to answer these questions, let us look first at the reasons for writing in the world outside the classroom. 'Creative Writing', in the sense of an imaginative composition of a literary type, is not being discussed here. It poses problems of a different nature which are only rarely relevant to learners of another language.

In the case of notes written for the writer's own benefit the intended audience is the writer himself. Because of this, the writing of notes will differ clearly from many other types of written language in which the writer and reader are not the same person. What the writer of notes can assume is a large element of 'given' knowledge, shared information. The need, therefore, to ensure that the meaning of the message is totally explicit is not so intense as it would be in the case of a writer conveying information to a reader far removed in space or time. Even in this instance, however, if the time interval between the writing of the notes and the reading of them is longer than was anticipated, it can be difficult to interpret them, as many students know to their cost.

The problem, then, for the notemaker as well as for the writer who addresses his words to others, is one of making quite explicit what the writer intends the reader to understand. In written communication there can be no additional help in transmitting the writer's message by resort to the methods normal in conversation. These are gesture, facial expression, stress, intonation and occasional repetition of the utterance. For this reason, the writer is forced to ensure that the information he wishes to convey is clear and unambiguous.

Speakers are accustomed to operating in a mode of communication which is relatively loosely structured and which has necessarily built into it a considerable amount of redundancy, which ensures that the speaker's intention becomes clear; this is necessary, since speech is transient; the actual sound cannot (unless it is recorded) be referred to after its original transmission.

Writing is different, since it has the advantage of being permanent. If the reader forgets by the end of a sentence how it began, he can refer back but still only to the same words. Although the reader is engaged in a form of dialogue with the writer, the writer is constrained by being committed to the one form in which he writes his message down. There is no possibility of repeating the message later, perhaps using slightly different words, as there is in speech. This is why he must be completely sure that he has expressed his meaning clearly the first time around.

It is important to notice here that neither written nor spoken language is in any way 'better' than the other. It is simply different. Anyone who has tried to make sense of a written transcription of a conversation (look again at the examples on pages 45 and 46) or who has listened to a talk being read from a prepared script, will be aware of the inherent unsuitability of the speech style for the written medium. Each style, or rather set of styles, evolved in the medium in which it normally occurs and is thus better suited to it.

5.3 Importance given to errors in writing

In the written medium, information has to be transmitted without any aid from sources other than the language itself. It seems to follow from this that more attention needs to be paid to the language as a code — in short, to the grammatical and lexical systems — than is the case with speech. When writing was the only way of storing information, it was vital that people should be educated to construct grammatically acceptable sentences and be able to spell correctly. Different dialects may be understandable in speech but the majority of grammars of English have been based on the 'standard' language. Because of this, a great deal of attention has traditionally been given to writing and errors in the medium tend to be regarded as indicative of some type of failure. Here, even more so than with speech, there is a danger that the language learner will tend to focus on the errors rather than on the presumed aim of the piece of writing: communication. Many teachers of English as a mother tongue now tend to regard fluency and the ability to manipulate the spoken and written language as higher in priority than a slavish adherence to rules of spelling. This attitude may be useful for the teacher of foreign or second languages as well, but what is probably more important is helping the students to avoid making errors in the first place.

5.4 Preparation of the learner for writing

It is probably more true with writing even than with speech that, if a student makes a large number of errors, he has not been adequately taught to do what he is attempting. In writing, above all, learners need careful preparation for their tasks. Look at this short paragraph which was written by a candidate taking a school leaving certificate examination:

'My favourite sport is football. I prefere it to others because as I am playing it. the inner part of the body specially lungs and heart (will have suficient) I fill it when the bloode is pumped it irritates and all dirt from the chest will be removed down to the stomach, will be out. that is not only for blood pressure, but body muscle will be strength no fatigue will happen during a long walking!'

This is a fairly extreme but genuine case. It would not be so very difficult for most teachers to indicate the points which need correcting. Spelling would receive attention, as would punctuation and syntax. The choice of 'dirt' is also unusual. It is interesting to note that the writing here, where the parenthesis occurs, takes on some of the characateristics of the normal spoken language; a sentence was started which the writer felt he could not continue, but instead of deleting or erasing the offending portion, he simply bracketed it. Even once the glaring spelling and grammatical mistakes have been indicated, there is still an area which clearly needs attention.

Let us consider the word 'that' (line 5); what does this word refer to? Football? The whole of the preceding statement? Or the blood being pumped around the system? Correction of written work often stops at the sentence level but one point of any written discourse is that there are links in it which refer from one sentence to another, and which give the whole passage an air of being one piece of material. Where these links are clearly successful, the passage has an air of unity and clarity and there is little ambiguity. But where these characteristic links are not clear in their reference, backwards or forwards, the meaning becomes obscured. The actual grammar may be correct, but the teacher is apt to underline such areas and indicate something is wrong by writing a word such as 'expression' next to them. One thing is clear: in the example from an exam paper, these devices for providing a coherent paragraph are not clearly used. In the first line, we assume 'others' would refer to 'sports', but the word 'sports' is not used in the passage. Further on, the repeated 'it' seems to refer to different antecedents, again not specified.

Since this kind of fault occurs frequently in learners' writing, it is advisable for teachers to draw attention to this feature of any written text when it is being treated in class. This is also the reason why it is much more useful for learners to work with either genuine but simplified texts which have these linking devices in them, or good made-up texts which also have them, rather than with exercises with separate sentences only.

TRAINING STUDENTS TO WRITE CONNECTED PROSE

Here are suggestions for two types of exercise which can be used to increase learners' awareness of linking devices.

1

> Below you will find a number of sentences. Arrange them into the best order. Pay particular attention to the linking words and words which refer back to other words in making your arrangement.
>
> 1 A car then had to swerve to miss her.
> 2 An old lady was crossing the road.
> 3 But the bus driver had seen what was happening.
> 4 She stopped to pick it up.
> 5 There was nearly a bad accident at the corner of Red Lion Square today.
> 6 Suddenly a gust of wind blew her hat off.
> 7 It narrowly avoided crashing into a bus.

2 An exercise on discourse linkers and functions from Widdowson (1980:43).

> WAYS OF ORDERING INFORMATION IN DESCRIPTIVE PASSAGES
>
> MILK PROCESSING
>
> Milk is first received at the milk plant where three different operations are performed on it: grading, weighing and sampling. It is graded by examining it for abnormal odours and flavours. The milk is weighed by emptying it into a tank on scales. A sample of the milk is then taken and tested for butterfat.
>
> The milk then flows to a clarifier whose purpose is to remove foreign material and sediment. The clarified milk may then be homogenized to prevent cream formation. The homogenized milk is then pasteurized to destroy all pathogenic bcteria. The pasteurized milk is cooled to 50°F or below. The cooled milk is then ready for distribution.

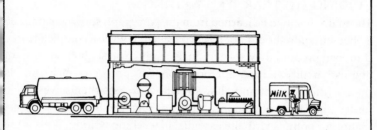

1 Using information in paragraph 1, complete this diagram to show the operations performed on milk.

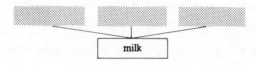

milk

2 Using information in paragraph 2, complete this diagram to show each stage and its purpose.

THEME   STAGE   PURPOSE

milk ────────────→

clarified milk ──────→

homogenized milk ──→

pasteurized milk ────→

cooled milk ──────→

Other examples of similar exercises, designed to teach writing, are to be found in another book in this series by Anita Pincas (1982) and in the three Student's Workbooks which accompany it.

GUIDING THE LEARNER'S WRITING

The main lesson to be learned from the paragraph shown on page 66 is that students should not be encouraged to write a completely free composition until they are genuinely ready to do so, both in terms of linguistic ability and concept formation. An approach which controls their written output and allows them to express themselves while under some form of guidance, either as regards structure or subject matter, or both, is virtually essential in teaching writing. (This is the basic approach throughout Pincas 1982, in the same series as this book.) For example, as an initial stage the students could simply be involved in answering questions in a certain order. This in itself would produce a short ordered statement:

Where do you live?   I live at _____.
How far is that from your school?   It is only _____ kilometres from my school.
How do you come to school every day?   I _____ to school every day.
How long does it take you? It takes me _____.
etc.

An alternative approach, perhaps for younger students, is simply to offer the opportunity of making choices from among several alternatives:

At the weekend I help my	father brother mother friends	to	gather the crops. do his homework. work in the house. paint their house.

A technique for more advanced students is to give a model paragraph on a topic, ask the students to find alternative lexical items which can be substituted for the original words. For example:

a   b

<u>Middleton</u> is a large <u>town</u>. It has <u>fifty thousand</u> inhabitants, many of

whom work in the local shipyard. It is on the banks of the river Ooze,
which flows into the Langton Channel. It has a small airport, two
railway stations and a coach terminal.

Edgington... a. city   b. two hundred thousand   c. iron and steel-
works   d. river Dovey   e. Irish Sea   f. bus station   g. passenger ferries   h. railway junction

Gradually more freedom can be given to the students by reducing
the amount of material to be copied. Further examples of this type of
work can be found in Moody 1968.

5.5   Correcting written errors

It was suggested earlier in this book that when students make errors
they do not necessarily learn those forms. There is, nevertheless,
much to be said for limiting the learner's opportunity to produce
errors in writing, if only because the conventions of writing are more
constricting and we are much less able to tolerate deviation from the
code. A further reason why it is better to avoid errors in written work
in the first place is that it is very disheartening to student and teacher
alike for a piece of work to be returned covered in red ink.

CHECKING WORK IN GROUPS OR PAIRS
When considering correction of errors at the stage of more or less
'free' writing, it is a useful and stimulating exercise for the students
to check their work in groups or pairs. This saves the teacher's time
and encourages communication amongst the students. If possible,
correction work should be conducted in English. Students should be
seated in such a way that it is easy for them to converse with each
other while they look at each others' books. A group of four is

convenient and allows quite a large number of communication possibilities (see Figure 7.)

Figure 7 Communication in groups of four

INTEGRATED SKILLS ACTIVITIES

In written work it is even easier than with oral work to focus on breaches of the language code and to adopt the attitude that students' errors are due to carelessness. Such an attitude usually then leads to the student being instructed to write out the corrected form several times as a 'punishment'. As this procedure provides no context for the language and demands no intellectual or emotional involvement on the part of the learner, it usually has little effect.

When a teacher feels that corrective work is necessary, the treatment will be much more successful if the written exercise involves the learner in activities that use all the language skills.

Here is an example of an 'integrated skills' activity. A teacher 'inherits' a class at the beginning of the term and discovers that comparative forms are generally wrongly used. The teacher re-teaches the comparative, using fairly mechanical exercises taken from any book that the learners are not already familiar with, then devises a role-play exercise in which the comparative can be used realistically.

The actual subject matter of the role-play depends very much on the level of the learners and on their previous experience and cultural background. One example is a role play on the construction of a new airport for a particular city or town. A major part of this incorporates rival firms making bids — which are *more* or *less* suitable; the materials would be *cheaper* or *dearer*, the specifications of the airport also differ. The runway could be *longer* or *shorter*. The depth of concrete used for the runways might *not be deep enough* to support a jumbo jet. Clearly this role-play would involve some preparation on the part of the teacher, but reports of the various groups would include a lot of comparison. Some groups could represent companies operating within cash and material limits set by the teacher and others could form various groups representing the council, the environment group, inhabitants and so on. A final class report could then be worked out in the form, say, of a newspaper article.

For teachers or students who would be very ill at ease with a role-play, a rather more 'mechanical' idea is to build up a stock of exercises taken from different text books. This is time-consuming initially but when the 'bank' exists, it can be used over and over again.

USING A CORRECTING CODE

When the teacher himself is correcting work (rather than students correcting each other's), it may well be found more profitable to concentrate on errors which are in the areas the class has been working on, rather than to indicate every single deviation. The difficulty here is for the teacher to assess the relative importance of errors. Chapter 6 will examine this point. Many teachers have found a profitable approach to correction in the use of a 'code' of indications written in margins or over the error. For example, **T** (tense), **WF** (word form), **WO** (word order), **S** (syntax), **A** (agreement), **V** (vocabulary), **Sp** (spelling), **P** (punctuation), **Art** (article), **R** (reference unclear), **St** (style), etc.

The advantage of this system is that it will lead the learners, if they are given adequate time, to work out for themselves what is wrong, and to go some way towards correcting it. But it should be stressed here that given adequate preparation and discussion, both with the teacher and with fellow students, learners should not be in the position of the writer of the example on page 66 of finding the initial task too difficult for them.

Here is an example of a student essay which has been corrected using a 'code' system.

Imagine that you were alone on an island

I am alone on an island. When I got up I was on a beach. I was all wat and I was very hungrey too. So I walked toward a forest. I saw there was many fruit trees. But there were no any fruit on it. I was very tried but I still wanted to find some food. Well, at last I found some potatoes under the ground. After I had eaten it I felt asleep under a trees. I was dreamt of my ship which had sank last night. Next morning I got up and saw little monkey. It looked like very funny so I used my hand to catch it, but it did not run away. I

> gave a potato to it. The monkey
> eat it very fast. After that it played
> with me and climbed up a tree and
> I folowed it. *(Sp)*

Key :	T – Tense	Ag – Agreement
	Sp – Spelling	S – Syntax
	Wf – Word form	Art – Article

What arises immediately from this system of correction is the question of categorising the deviation. For example, the word 'sank' in line 11 has been marked as a spelling problem. But it could be a grammatical one. Similarly with 'felt' on line 9; is the 't' merely a slip of the pen (a lapse) or is this how the learner would pronounce the word?

At a later stage of learning, some teachers go further than this and simply give references to grammar or class books where the particular point which the student has misproduced is dealt with. This is a very useful and time saving technique for the busy teacher!

5.6 Influence of context on writing style

One of the features of the writing exercise, once our students have attained the free composition stage, is the problem mentioned earlier of a distant audience and the purpose of the communication. Most language courses (and examinations) now avoid de-contextualised discussion questions such as 'To be or not to be — discuss'. Learners are better motivated when they are given work in a recognisable context, but, to avoid stylistic anomalies, learners need to be shown examples of the particular style appropriate to the exercise they are engaged in. The language forms of an informal letter will differ from those used in an application for a job; these in turn will not bear much resemblance to an advertisement for, say, a second-hand bicycle or a report of a chemistry experiment. The problem of style is important if we are to avoid the type of writing found in some English language newspapers published in areas where English is used as a second language, where styles are mixed to an alarming degree, occasionally with unintentionally unfortunate results: 'Mum and two kids die in smash'.

But the provision of an (imagined?) audience is also a help to the writer not just with regard to style, but also to the actual information he can assume as known. For example, compare these three exercise titles:

1 Write a letter describing your last holiday.
2 Write a letter to a friend in a nearby town describing your last holiday
3 Write a letter to a friend in a foreign country describing what you did during your last holiday.

The first title is likely to lead to more problems, since the writer must work out for himself a suitable set of 'knowns' in his supposed audience. In the second title, the writer can assume a common stock of cultural knowledge. In the third, no cultural knowledge can be supposed so more basic information will need to be given.

5.7 Writing as an aid to learning

Many students' introduction to writing occurs well before they are required to begin a course of composition writing, however controlled it may be. Writing is used in the early stages of learning to aid the 'consolidation' of the learning. After the introduction of some new material and opportunities to practise it and perhaps to use it in slightly less controlled conditions, the learner writes some form of exercise, frequently as homework. Since no-one's memory is perfect, however much practice the student has been able to carry out, there is always a chance of error creeping into even this type of rather elementary work. Once again, prevention seems better than cure, since once a form appears in writing, it acquires permanence and can be referred to again, leading to a familiarity with an 'undesirable' form.

Ideally in this situation, where the learner is consolidating, he will have little to do that is new to him, thus reducing the chance of an error. A careful approach to writing should be cultivated in learners, thus reducing also the chance of mistakes and lapses. Plenty of time should be allowed here for checking or 'self-monitoring'. Once again, working in pairs can be of use. But here, above all, a teacher's approach to the correction of deviant forms, whether systematic or not, needs to be selective, with the main effort and attention being devoted to the point being consolidated.

For example, in this case the teacher has asked pupils to write out for homework an exercise that has been done in class which is focusing on the simple past tense forms of some verbs.

> In the picture we saw <u>meny</u> things. A little boy <u>kiked</u> a ball into the street. A car skidded to miss the ball. It crashed <u>in</u> a shop window. A window cleaner fell <u>of</u> a ladder. A motor cyclist fell <u>of</u> his bike. Another car <u>stoped</u> suddenly to miss the <u>moter</u> cyclist. A third car bumped into the <u>cecond</u> car. <u>Too</u> women <u>run</u> to help the drivers of the car and the motor cyclist.

Clearly there are a number of points worth comment here. For a start, it would appear that the teacher could have given more assistance and perhaps prevented some of the deviant forms. However, to remove the focus of attention from the teaching point would be a mistake. The spelling errors, in so far as they are systematic ('litle' and 'stoped' both have the double letter wrong, and 'kiked' could possibly be related to the same systematic error) could be noted and treated at a more appropriate time, as could the again apparently systematic 'fall of', possibly together with 'crash in'. The anomalous spellings 'moter' and 'cecond' could probably be ignored altogether as they are almost certainly not systematic. The form 'motor' actually occurs in its correct form on the previous line, so we can assume that 'moter' is a mistake; similarly with 'cecond', formed perhaps by analogy with words like 'ceiling' which led the learner to think 'ce' = 's', but this is more likely to be simply a slip or lapse.

It would appear that this particular pupil attempts to spell by sound-a common strategy. 'Meny' too, and more seriously, 'run', would appear to be examples of this. The errors which need immediate treatment then and further work in the form of controlled writing (see Pincas 1982) are: 'kiked', 'stoped', 'run'. The last form here 'run', is the most serious error, since it could possibly involve a misunderstanding about the spoken form if the student is really spelling more or less phonetically. This student would therefore need more oral practice. The other forms would not be obviously wrong if spoken, but written practice would help the spelling. Many teachers, presented with this piece of work, would only mark as incorrect the forms they intend to discuss and work on later.

Summary

1   Writing needs to be much more explicit than speech because communication is dependent on the words alone and the writer and reader may be far removed in space or time. Even for the

native speaker the written form of a language is harder to manipulate effectively than the spoken form.

2　Writing can be an aid to memory. Students should be prevented from making errors in writing by being given a great deal of guidance in the early stages and not being asked to do exercises they have not been sufficiently prepared for.

3　Peer-checking can save the teacher time and develop a new channel of learning for the students.

4　Where work is corrected by the teacher, a code which indicates to the learners the type of error they have made will involve them in more conscious assessment of what they have produced.

5　The appropriate style for a written communication is determined by its context. Students will gain confidence in their handling of the written language if they are given practice in using the language in realistic situations that draw on a combined use of all the language skills.

6 Techniques of error analysis

An error analysis can give a picture of the type of difficulty learners are experiencing. If carried out on a large scale such a survey can be helpful in drawing up a curriculum. For the class teacher an error analysis can give useful information about a new class. In a class – or country – with different first languages, it can indicate problems common to all and problems common to particular groups. If two or three surveys are carried out at intervals of time, the teacher can begin to build up a profile of each individual's problems and see to what extent his grasp of the target language is improving. By using error analysis as a monitoring device, the teacher can assess more objectively how his teaching is helping his students.

This kind of analysis can be made of either spoken or written language. Speech would, of course, have to be recorded in some way, say on a cassette recorder, to allow the teacher time to examine it. The approach used would have to differ in the case of speech: if the teacher had recorded a group or groups undertaking a communicative task, then the usual repetitions, blends, restatements of sentences etc, would have to be taken into account, and only gross errors and mistakes noted. Identifying pronunciation errors is not a simple matter either. If the utterance has apparently been clearly understood by the person to whom it was made then probably any error in it is not important.

6.1 The mechanics of error analysis

As to the actual mechanics of an error analysis, there are fundamentally two main approaches. The first, and more common one, is to set up one's categories of error, based on a set of preconceptions about the learner's most common problems. The second is to group the errors as they are collected into particular areas of grammatical and semantic problems. The drawback of the first approach is that the issue is prejudged; errors will be found to fill categories, and the investigation takes on a certain circularity, since errors can be sorted out only in terms of predetermined error types. An administrative advantage of this type of survey, however, is that it is easier and quicker to carry out, since errors are simply indicated as ticks on a list of categories. The second approach has the advantage of allowing the errors themselves to determine the categories chosen; by a process of sorting and re-sorting (the errors need to be copied onto cards for this process) the categories will eventually define themselves.

Examples of three different methods of carrying out an error analysis follow. The first is based on the first of the main approaches outlined above. The other two examples are based on the second type of approach.

1 THE 'PRE-SELECTED CATEGORY' APPROACH
Etherton (1977) suggests the following list of headings for *starting* the work of classifying errors. He suggests refinements to be made later by the teacher to suit the material fed into the analysis.

List of headings

Abbreviations
Adjectives
Adverbials
Age
Agreement
American English
  (ie *not* wrong)
Apostrophe
Articles *a*, *an*

Articles (omitted)
Articles (unnecessary,
  but inserted)
Articles (wrong one used)
as
be
can
Capital letters
Comma
Comparison

Conditionals	Possessive adjectives
Conjunctions	Prepositions (omitted)
could	Prepositions (unnecessary but
Days and date	inserted)
Direct questions	Prepositions (wrong one)
do	Present Continuous
ed/ing	Present Participle
Full stop	Present Perfect
Future Perfect	Punctuation
Gerund	Question tags
have	Reflexive pronouns
Hyphen	Relative pronouns
Indirect questions	*'s'* not needed
Indirect speech	Sequence of tenses
Infinitive	Simple Future
Inverted commas	Simple Past
make	Simple Past, passive
must	Simple Present
Nouns (countable/	Simple Present, passive
uncountable)	Slang
nt/nce	Spelling
Numbers	Spelling (pronunciation)
one word or two?	Spelling (L₁ interference)
Passive	Spelling (metathesis)
Past Continuous	*There is/are*
Past Participle	Time
Past Perfect	Unclassified
Personal pronouns	Verbs — past not known
Plural problems	Vocabulary

Etherton makes some important points in his summary. First, he
indicates that it is important that the material from which the errors
are taken is as representative of the student's standard of work as
possible. It must also be *free writing*; guided writing will only allow

certain errors and those may not be a representative selection, though it may be that teachers will wish to check on errors produced in guided writing too. (This approach, however, would be rather cumbersome for that type of exercise.)

Second, teachers will find the collection they make more flexible if the entries are cross referenced from one section to another, for example:

Error   *I saw the man was died*

3 cards are needed:
1 died   (Stored alphabetically in
2 dead   vocabulary section.)
3 'Pairs of words confused'
   ('Front' card, with actual examples kept behind it.)

Third, Etherton points out that even a fairly simple collection of errors can indicate where either the teacher's work is not proving effective, or the syllabus itself is defective either as to the ordering of, or failure to include, certain language items.

2 'LET THE ERRORS DETERMINE THE CATEGORIES'

This is the final list of error types arrived at by Hudson (1971) by the process of recording errors onto separate cards, one error per card, and then grouping the cards together in boxes. Gradually the sorting produced smaller and smaller groups, until eventually all the cards were accounted for apart from a handful, which appear in the final two categories in this list.

Tense
    for example, simple past instead of simple present active
    A brother has more strength to help me whenever I fought with anyone.
    Agreement
        For example, subject - verb agreement
    . . .*things which makes me happy*

Determiners
  For example, omission of the definite article
  Before United States . . .
Word order
  For example, adverbs
  They might have also some reason . . .
Subordinate clauses
  For example, relative clauses
  . . . the only boy what my mother has.
Ungrammatical redundancy
  For example, redundant adverbs
  We returned back to Addis Ababa . . .
Fragments
  For example, *When he sat down. . .*
Possessive and attributive structures
  For example, *of* construction instead of *'s*
  The only son of my mother . . .
Incomplete structures
  For example, obligatory object omitted
  'One can enjoy with a brother.
Comparative constructions
Superlative constructions
Reported speech
  For example, failure to make adjustments in pronouns and time-words.
Negative constructions
Structural idioms
  For example, infinitive instead of *ing* after various verbs.
  They don't mind to accept it.
Participial phrases
  I was left there being lonely and miserable.
Parallel structures
  For example, present participle with non-finite verb.
  . . . seeing my family and went for a picnic.

Pronouns, infinitives and infinitive constructions
Non-referential *There* sentence
   They were many men who were drinking heavily.
Derivation
   For example, noun derivation
   . . . the day of happy.
Lexical selections
   For example prepositions
   . . . who lives at this world.
So . . . that construction (miscellaneous errors)
Spelling
Capitalisation
Punctuation
Handwriting
Style
Miscellaneous unclassifiable errors
Miscellaneous complex and irreducible errors

This approach is suitable only for written English. It is recommended that all the errors/mistakes which the teacher records should be on cards rather than in an exercise book. Cards can easily be re-ordered and recategorised, whereas the pages of an exercise book cannot easily be moved, and may become full too soon to accommodate all the entries a teacher wishes to make. If cards are difficult to obtain, then separate small pieces of paper are just as mobile, if not quite so durable. Cards from different levels or age-groups of students should be kept apart, as errors clearly change over time.

First, the error/mistake should be sorted out from its immediate context. For example, when several overlapping 'deviations' occur, they need to be isolated. Look at this sentence: 'My sister and me are wanting brother.' For this, three cards need to be made. Only one error will appear on each card, thus:

Card 1   My sister and I want —— brother.
Card 2   My sister and *me* want a brother.

Card 3   My sister and I *are wanting* a brother.

The deviation can be underlined on the card for ease of reference later. Card 1 would be categorised under 'Determiner' (the indefinite article 'a' is omitted). The second card would be assigned to 'Pronoun'. (The form here should be 'I'.) The third card would be assigned to a category under 'Tense'. (The present continuous tense has been used in place of the normal present simple.)

   The disadvantage of this method is that it is time-consuming. On the other hand, all the cards can be kept and checked later (assuming there is sufficient storage space to allow this!).

3   THE 'QUICK CHECK' APPROACH

This method is more likely to be commonly used by classroom teachers who wish to check quickly whether or to what extent their teaching material has been learnt by their classes. This technique could be used for either speech or writing, whereas the other two approaches described in this chapter are really only suitable for the written language. In order to check the students' spoken language, the teacher should listen to the language used in an activity which is designed to produce particular forms. For example, the students can be given a pair work exercise where they are required to find their 'partner' by asking simple questions such as 'What is your name?', 'What do you do for a living?'. (Cards giving the relevant information are given out before the activity starts. See Revell 1979:15 for more details.)

   In an activity such as this teachers may particularly wish to note the tense being used (the present simple) or the pronoun forms. They can note on a checklist where the errors occur and, given sufficient time, note what they are. But the main aim here is to note quickly the correct or incorrect use of recently taught forms. Figure 8 shows an example of a checklist.

   The checklist gives the teacher an idea as to the ratio of correct to incorrect forms. This is, of course, easier at the lower levels of

Present Simple Tense	Pronoun Forms	Verb/ Subject Agreement	Vocabulary Misused
✓	✓	✗	bakes
✓	✓	✗	
✓	✓	✗	
✗ (be)	✓	✗	
✗ (be)	✓	✓	
✓		✓	

Comments: In the main, not bad. Verb/subject
agreement needs more work.
Pronouns seem well known.
Pres. Simp. of 'be' gives some
difficulties—re-teach

Figure 8. Teacher's checklist of Correct and Incorrect Forms

teaching. Higher up the range, it is easier for students to avoid using language items they are not certain about; in other words, to express what they need to say in ways other than those the teacher is hoping to check. If this avoidance is done easily and at no great loss to the students' ability to communicate meaning, then this, too, is a useful skill for the students and can be ticked on the checklist.

6.2 Uses of error analysis

DANGERS
There is a danger in using these types of survey that too much attention will then be given to trying to blot out certain characteristic errors, leaving no time for other, perhaps equally useful parts of the language. For example, let us imagine that in a nationwide analysis performed on a sample of examination papers, a tendency is discovered for learners to use the present simple tense instead of the normal past simple. For example:

a   After I had waited for an hour, my friends come.
b   When we reached home, I thank him.

However, if a lot of valuable class time is given over to the attempted prevention of this type of error, there is less time available for other useful items. Each teacher needs to draw up his own scale of priorities based on the students' envisaged need for the language they are learning. If we remember that any language is a system, which is itself comprised of many different systems (grammatical, phonological and semantic and their sub-systems) then we are better placed to realise that simply eradicating one error or set of errors is not in itself likely to help our learners actually to improve their capacity to use the language for communicative purposes.

CONTRASTIVE ANALYSIS
We cannot now make the 'strong' claims for contrastive and error

analyses that were popular some years ago. These were that analyses would indicate areas of first language interference, thus informing teachers of items in the syllabus deserving special emphasis, or even what items should be taught. (See page 28 for a discussion of contrastive analysis.) Although this strong 'predictive' claim for contrastive analysis can hardly be sustained any longer, it is certainly true to say that analysis has a useful explanatory role. That is, it can still be said to explain certain errors and mistakes. For example, the author came across the word 'extray' in a piece of written work by a Maltese student. Although the meaning may be clear from the context, it is quite helpful to the teacher to know that the English sound æ is usually pronounced as something similar to ε in Malta, as this is the closest Maltese sound; and in Maltese spelling, 'x' is the symbol for the ʃ sound. So it is easy to see how 'ashtray' became 'extray'.

INVESTIGATING COMMUNICATIVE STRATEGIES

We can also say that sampling a group's output over a period of time can give the teacher an idea about common and particular problems and the development of the group through a series of 'interlanguages' (see Chapter 2). The surveys would be interpreted, it is hoped, in order to investigate the communicative strategies used by learners to express their meanings in the target language as well as to establish a set of points for 'remedial work'.

'Investigating the communicative strategies' means examining the language the learners use in order to convey their meaning. This can take the form of avoiding certain structures or vocabulary items, generally those which the learners feel uncertain about, and/or using other language items more than one would expect. It can also take the form of using the resources of language that are known to the learner to help him express what he may not yet have learnt. In this particular case, where a learner is struggling to express a meaning, he may well turn to a language better known to him: his L_1 or a better known L_2, giving rise to L_1 transfer. For example, a French speaker of

English who has not learnt the present perfect continuous tense will typically produce the form: 'I am staying in England since the 1st May'. In French the present tense is used to convey the meaning of the English expression 'I have been staying . . .'

MONITORING PROGRESS

It is important to remember that one analysis from a piece of written work is likely to produce only part of the picture. The topic(s) of the exercise may show up errors in the use of a particular language form because that is the form that needs to be used for the topic. Other errors may be masked because they are excluded by the topic.

Here, for example, is a fairly typical list of topics:

1 Two customs you would like to change and why.
2 Describe the happiest day of your life, saying what it was that made you happy.
3 You have been offered a free trip to a foreign country.
  Give your reasons for the country which you choose.
4 You see an accident in the street. Make a statement to a policeman.

In writing on these topics there would be very few, if any, opportunities to use the present continuous tense, so the errors in that form would appear few; on the other hand in questions 2 and 4 the predominant tenses would be past simple with, perhaps in number 4, some examples of the past continuous ('While I was walking down the street...', 'While the driver was talking to his passenger...' etc). The reverse of this problem is also true; namely that, for example, in question 3, there is likely to be some misuse of the present simple tense, since it occurs in the title ('I think I choose Japan because...').

The teacher must also be aware of the fact that it is generally possible to avoid parts of the language, grammatical or semantic, which one is not certain of. This is hardly surprising; native speakers of a language use this device themselves. The teacher should think carefully about what he is trying to discover about the learner's command of a language by asking him to write a composition on a given topic. Does he wish to discover which items of the language the student has not learnt or rather how successfully he can use the language resources at his command to express his ideas? The student may well play safe by only using the language he is sure of but if the exercise has been set as a diagnostic tool, then the teacher wants to encourage non-defensive language behaviour and use the data from the error analysis to discover further areas which need teaching or re-teaching.

What an error analysis can never do is to tell us how to go about ensuring that our students do, in fact, learn what we hope they will. H V George (1972:62) remarks that one of the most useful forms of treatment of errors may well be to tolerate them, since they represent incomplete knowledge of the language system, and time spent by the student on correcting errors is time not spent on further exposure to the language. This further exposure it just as likely to assist the learner in his move towards the control he needs as is a mechanical copying out of correct forms. Teachers must use their own judgment on this point. With some language items it is vital to ensure that the correct forms are being used before going on to cover new material because these forms occur so frequently in the language. For example, if some forms of the verb 'to be' are being produced incorrectly these need to be corrected early as they need to be used with other grammatical structures.

6.3 Problems in analysing errors

There may be times when one judge or teacher will consider a given form an error, while another would be consider it acceptable. Since language constantly changes and develops, what is considered 'incorrect' today may be acceptable tomorrow. Despite Dr Johnson's opposition (he considered the word slang, and would not include it in his famous dictionary), 'job' is now a perfectly 'correct' English word. Quite apart from the problem of acceptability versus grammaticality, there are also areas of idiom where an awkwardness may or may not be considered 'incorrect'.

Here are three examples which may sound unusual, but were eventually accepted in a major error analysis (Hudson 1971):

a   All this was done *for the progress* of my country.
b   ...and *it is always my prayer* that my country will develop ...
c   They had come to *help me to celebrate* my birthday.

Many teachers would claim that the forms in italics are incorrect, as they are 'simply translations from the learners' own languages'. This surely cannot be a valid reason for not accepting them, since there almost certainly will be occasions when the use of this very natural communicative 'strategy' (of translating from L_1) results in acceptable English sentences.

Central to this issue, and indeed to the notion of error in general, is the teacher's own view of language and grammar. Such areas as sequence of tenses ('After we ate, we continued to talk . . .'), the use of commas ('Now that my sister is four years old, she often tells us ...') are well known problem areas, since they are somewhat ill-defined. On the other hand, examining boards quite often have very firm views on what is correct, and it is in these areas that learners need to be made aware that while we may *say* 'After we *ate*, we continued to talk', it is always safer to *write* a past perfect tense in this context, thus: 'After we *had eaten*, we continued ...'

Further problems in classification of errors do not necessarily relate to the teacher's view of language, but rather, his interpretation of the nature of the error. For example, when a learner writes 'chose' for 'choose', how is this to be classified? It could be regarded as spelling (by analogy possibly, with 'lose') or as an incorrect tense. There are other errors of this type which are familiar to most teachers: man/men, run/ran, loose/lose, etc. All that can be done is to use the context to arrive at some interpretation, or, even better if possible, to ask the learner what he thought he had written. Again, the type of error involving count nouns poses problems: 'The police came to my house. I told him …' Is this an omission of 'man' after 'police' or an error in the agreement between the noun and the subsequent pronoun?

Despite these problems, however, some form of analysis of the learners' output, especially if repeated on roughly comparable tasks, can be of use to the teacher, both from the point of view of the teacher's interest in his learners' development and secondly, and perhaps more importantly, to enable him to discover where his teaching has not resulted in students' learning.

6.4 Procedure for Remedial Teaching

This section indicates how a teacher might use the information gained from a rather basic error analysis. The exercise (on the topic of 'Problems of the Third World') was written by a fourteen-year-old German student learning English in a secondary school in Germany. The teacher has marked the mistakes/errors and made notes on which points need to be corrected in class.

The poor peoples have a shortage of food. They live isolate from stress. There life expectasion is small because they have not food. Often they have many children and so they have a big familie to feed. For example: In India there is not adequate food for population and many peoples starve. There subistance is bad. They often live in slums ∧ this are area of damps dark and

cold and the flats are dirty. They
have not enough money for gas.
Often they get not food for survival.
They have not learnt anything and
their expectations are small.

Main areas of error: 1. Verb + negative
                       2. People / peoples
                       3. Their / there

Here is a suggested procedure for remedying the mistakes/errors noted by the teacher.

1 Verb + Negative

a   Demonstrate the errors on board:

* they get not food

*they eat not enough …

*the poor people live not well …

etc.

b   Demonstrate methods of making verbs negative:

> I like chocolates.
>
> My sister <u>does not like</u> them.
>
> Lions eat meat.
>
> Giraffes <u>do not eat</u> meat.

Explanation

In statements, if the affirmative verb is a simple tense form, use 'do' or 'did' (past tense) and the infinitive without 'to', and put 'not' between the two words. The two exceptions to this are the verbs 'be' and 'have' when it is used as an auxiliary or when it shows possession or some closely related idea. 'Can', 'may', 'must', 'ought', 'need' are also treated as auxiliaries, with 'not' placed immediately after them:

The house *is not* very large

The roof *is not* waterproof

The town *had no* water

We *have not seen* him for several days

We *cannot* buy any food today

etc.

(It would be worth mentioning that the formerly American English 'We do not have any bananas' is becoming increasingly common in British English.)

c.   The work could continue with further details on making verbs negative, for example, in questions. (Since space is limited, this is not dealt with in detail here.) The next stage in the process is for the teacher to get the student to produce orally and in writing some correct examples of negative sentences using a substitution table. This work will be largely mechanical, although teachers should, naturally, try to contextualise it as far as possible, using, say, pictures, or real life situations. These tables are adapted from George 1967:12 and 13.

1	2	3	4	5
That Her Her mother's Her sister's	pink orange pale yellow white blue new old	saree blouse dress coat skirt veil	looked nice suited her fitted her looks nice suits her fits her	
	pretty gay bright faded spotted striped		does not did	look nice suit her fit her

1	2	3	4	5
This That	type kind sort colour style pattern model fashion	did not didn't doesn't does not	suit go with look well with seem proper with match	her hair style her other things her complexion

d The next stage in the remedial process is simple completion of sentences. For example:

1 Most children in developing countries (not, eat) enough . . .
2 Most Europeans (not, understand) what real poverty means . . .
3 The World Bank (not, have solved) the problems of aid to the Third World . . .

Stages c and d SHOULD BE COMPLETED QUICKLY.

e Activity: 'Questionnaires'.

(For a full description of this activity, see Revell 1979:42ff.)

This activity ensures that students have a chance to use both affirmative and negative forms while concentrating on content.

2 peoples/people

This area of error (and 'their/there') is not so central to language as the first error dealt with, so procedure for remedial work is not so detailed.

The difference between 'people' and 'peoples' could be explained in terms of national or ethnic groups versus the notion of humanity in general and some examples given, followed by some exercises in which the students are asked to choose the appropriate form.

3 their/there

This is purely a spelling error made, incidentally, by many L_1 children. After drawing the students' attention to this feature of

English spelling, some written practice showing the use of 'their' and 'there' in context would be enough.

Summary

1   The two basic approaches to error analysis both have their advantages and disadvantages. Three techniques of error analysis, illustrating these basic approaches, are described in the chapter.

2   The teacher must bear in mind the problems of finding impartial evidence of the students' level of competence. The errors, or lack of them, in a piece of work being analysed may be determined by the topic of the exercise or the learner's use of communication strategies.

3   Error analysis can be especially useful if repeated on comparable tasks with intervals of time in between. It gives the teacher an idea about how individual students are progressing through their interlanguage and indicates any points which have generally not been learned.

4   It should be stressed that remedial teaching carried out as a result of the findings of an error analysis should use a different approach from that tried for the initial teaching activity.

7 Communication and assessment problems

7.1 Errors and breakdown of communication

It is sometimes assumed by language learners that if they make any kind of error when talking to a native speaker of the language they are learning, they will either not be understood or will be derided in some way. The learner's frequent response to this is to maintain a terrified silence on meeting a native speaker. Two questions tend to run through the learner's mind: Will the native speaker fail to understand the learner's meaning if there are any deviations in his English? Will he think the learner is funny when he makes mistakes?

As far as the first question is concerned it is not in fact usual in conversation to listen more closely to *how* a speaker is expressing his meaning than to *what* the speaker is trying to communicate. Certain errors, of course, may lead to a breakdown in communication, others may lead to some rather more social reaction, such as faint annoyance (and more of this later), but generally, the listener is more concerned with the content of the message than with the code. The learner may find this hard to believe, especially if the setting for the conversation is the school classroom.

Imagine a situation where someone is walking through the shopping centre of his home town. He is approached by a foreigner who is lost and is looking for the bus station. If the foreigner asks the following question, 'Excuse, where is bus station?', the listener is *not* likely to reply, 'You should have said, "Excuse *me*," and "Where is *the* bus station?"', and simply walk away. The meaning of the question, although imperfectly expressed, is clear enough. The tourist will get his information, probably spoken more slowly and clearly than it would be if addressed to an obvious native speaker. (Paradoxically, if the tourist sounds too fluent, he may get an answer he cannot understand!)

OVERCOMING THE LEARNER'S FEAR OF ERROR

If the error does not *necessarily* lead to a breakdown in communication, where then, to look at the second of the two questions, does this widely held misconception arise? Two sources are proposed here, both resulting from a common classroom attitude to error. The first is the ridicule of the learner's classmates, or the memory of such ridicule in previous educational experience. Some adult learners are very reluctant to attempt any use of a new language for this reason. This itself arises from the second source of the learner's fear: the usual concentration in the classroom on the code rather than the message itself. That is, in less technical terms, the teacher's attention is concentrated on the grammar and vocabulary and not on the ideas being expressed in a learner's utterances.

This is only one good reason why learners need to have practice in using the foreign language for the passing on of information or opinions which are needed in some way. In the absence of the visiting native speaker, with whom contact is usually somewhat limited, other members of the class could be used for language activities carried out in groups or pairs. There are now many publications dealing with such activities which are easily available for the classroom teacher; some of these can be found in the suggestions for further reading.

Here is one example of this type of activity. A class of university lecturers who were improving their language skills and looking at English of a technical nature were given the following exercise: the class of sixteen were divided up into four groups of four, and each group was given one of a set of four posters on the subject of the British Royal National Lifeboat Institution. (See Figure 9.) Each group had to read and make sense of the information on the poster and make brief notes, then the groups changed around as illustrated.

Stage one groups

Class divides into 4 groups:

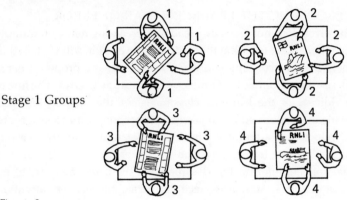

Stage 1 Groups

Figure 9

When discussion and note taking is finished, the class moves into stage two groups (See Figure 10.)

Stage two groups

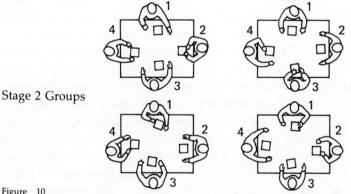

Stage 2 Groups

Figure 10

Each of the stage two groups is made up of one member of each of the stage one groups. They have between them all the necessary information.

After the formation of the new groups, the different information is shared by the new groups, each member making a short contribution which is noted by the others. Finally, there is a questionnaire to answer, which the groups can discuss as they answer it together (See Figure 11.)

This is, clearly, a technique that can be used with many different types of stimulus. The important aspect is that each of the original groups should only have part of the information. The amount of language preparation which precedes this type of exercise will depend very much on the level of the learners.

7.2 Relative gravity of errors

We should not be too idealistic about language teaching. As has been remarked elsewhere, if the teacher were to pay no attention at all to the learners' errors, then the students' chances of success in examinations would obviously be reduced. Communicative ability is also affected by too many errors if and when the opportunity comes. Since many schools and teachers judge both themselves and their peers by how well their students do in the exams, some attention needs to be given to erroneous forms. Many teachers have a 'scale of seriousness' of errors, and a certain amount of work has been done on this topic: error 'gravity'.

If asked which kind of error they would find 'more serious', most teachers would say 'grammar' rather than 'vocabulary' (or 'lexis'). It is the grammatical elements in a sentence which show the relationships of one part of a sentence to another. For example, the usual word order of a simple sentence in English is subject + verb + object (S+V+O). If this is changed to, say, V+S+O, then there will be severe problems of comprehension. (See also the

Sample questions on the RNLI Posters

1 In what century was the Lifeboat Service founded?

2 Where are the headquarters of the RNLI?

3 Is the Honorary Secretary paid?

4 How many men are there usually in a crew?

5 How many of the crew are paid for their work?

6 How much money does the Government give to the service?

7 What is a Blue Peter Boat?

8 Name three places that lifeboats may wish to communicate with.

9 What kinds of engines are used to drive lifeboats?

10 Besides sailing, crew members need training in other skills. Name one.

11 What signal is used to tell a crew that a ship is in trouble?

12 How many lives are saved on average per week?

13 Why might a boat need direction finding equipment?

14 Name any two special characteristics of lifeboats that seem important to you.

15 What is the range of speeds that lifeboats have?

Figure 11

global local' distinction on page 106.) Instead of 'The man saw the woman', we would have 'Saw the man the woman'. Now, instead of a statement, we could interpret this either as a question, or as a statement meaning either that the man saw the woman or the woman saw the man.

If we compare this type of error with, say, the replacement of the word 'desk' by 'table' in the sentence 'The man sat at the ....', which would alter the meaning but would not lead to possible complete misunderstanding, we can see that the grammatical error would appear as the more serious of the two, although the substitution of an incorrect vocabulary item can lead to *mis*understanding (that is, the listener may assume he has understood when, in fact, he has not done so) rather than a clear failure to understand.

What has been discussed here is error gravity in general. As far as each individual classroom teacher is concerned, the situation may well vary, depending on his aims and what has most recently been covered in the language course. The teacher may wish to indicate both for his own records of student performance and for the mark book the relative gravity of different errors by deducting, say, two marks for errors in a particular tense form, recently taught, while removing only one for other errors in the piece of work.

7.3 Error frequency

Frequency' — the number of times an error occurs — can be regarded in basically two ways. Firstly, the so-called 'absolute' frequency of an error (the number of times that the error occurs) and secondly, the number of times the error could have occurred, relative to the length of the piece of writing.

If a learner produces, for example, a piece of writing of two hundred and fifty words and makes ten errors, we can simply register the fact that the number of errors is ten, or we can calculate a relative frequency' by multiplying the number by one hundred and dividing the result by the total number of words written to obtain a percentage, thus: $\frac{100 \times 100}{250} = 4$ In this way, we can compare across pieces of work of differing lengths the relative number of errors. This measure is useful in comparing, say, pieces of writing of differing lengths.

Consistency is also considered important. Let us take two examples. One beginner writes (or produces orally) a piece of English in which the third person singular present simple tense 's' is omitted from every verb where it would normally occur. If we are to mark this piece of work, few, if any, teachers would consider penalising every instance of this error. On the other hand, if another learner sometimes omits the 's' and sometimes produces it, then there is more of a problem: should the teacher count every incorrect form as a separate error, or should this count only as one error? In psychological terms, the 'rule' that states 'add -s to the verb in the third person singular in the present simple tense' is only partly learned. Another possibility here is that the omissions, especially if few in number, are 'lapses' or 'mistakes' rather than errors, and that the learner, given the opportunity to revise his work could correct the forms; here the advantage of a code system of indicating incorrect forms becomes apparent again.

The frequency and consistency of errors has an obvious interest for the teacher. It is one sure source of information on whether or not an individual learner or group has mastered a 'rule' or not. It is by paying attention to the criteria or error gravity and frequency that the teacher will be able to plan rationally his remedial teaching.

7.4 Breaking 'major' and 'minor' rules

A further approach to error gravity involves rules and exceptions to rules. For example, the student in the previous example who had only partly learned the 'add -s to the verb in the third person singular present simple tense' rule might, as a result of his learning activities, produce the form 'he cans swim well', where the form of the 'modal' verb *can* constitutes an exception to the general rule. A different type of example would be when a learner produces the form 'childs' or 'sheeps' instead of 'children/sheep'. The general rule has been over-generalised to cover even forms which are normally not so treated. It is interesting to note here that it is exceptions to general rules which so often appear in very young native speakers' language in the overgeneralised form (see page 7).

In the event of teachers having to decide which is the more serious type of error, it would appear that infringing an exception to a rule, or a minor rule, would be less serious than transgressing a major rule. For example, producing the form 'childs' would not be so serious as consistently failing to add any plural endings to nouns.

A similar phenomenon to this one is to be seen where the learner has realised that a rule of some kind is operative; for example, the distinction in English between 'he' and 'she'. However, the learner may consistently use 'he' where a native speaker uses 'she' and 'she' where an English speaker would say 'he'. From a psychological point of view, he has realised the existence of the rule, but has confused the application of it. On the other hand, a learner who fails to make any distinction between the two forms has not even learnt that a rule exists.

It should be noted here that the seriousness of erroneous forms in terms of rules learnt or half learnt may not be the same as that involving a failure to communicate, leaving either doubt or actual misunderstanding in the listener's or reader's mind. The traditional bugbear of the English teacher, the omission of the 's' in the third person singular hardly affects communication in itself; it is a fact, though, that when such a basic rule has not been learnt, there is a strong chance that other rules are also being broken, and that if enough of the language is distorted, communication is likely to become difficult.

Besides distortion of the message, there is another factor which can be taken into account in deciding whether an error is a major or a minor one. This is the effect the error has on the relations between the speaker/writer and the listener/reader. Investigations have been carried out into the effects of irritation in the listener, brought about by errors. The more irritation in the listener, the more it could interfere with his attention to the meaning, and the more seriously would the error be regarded. The response of irritation to an error is, however, clearly subjective, and will depend on the listener's character, his experience of language learners, his attitude to the particular speaker ('a charming, elegant young lady' or 'a spoilt, rich little girl') and his educational background and his resultant degree of awareness of the problems of using a language other than one's own.

In a culture where great attention is paid to a prescribed form of the L_1, such as France, with its Académie Française, the attitude to deviation is likely to be much more strict than in a country with no such authoritative view, such as England.

Figure 12 shows in diagram form how to go about deciding whether an error is a major one or not and, if it is, what priority to give it in planning remedial treatment.

7.5 Global and local errors

Burt and Kiparsky (1972) have suggested a distinction in errors which relates to comprehensibility. They suggest fundamentally two types of error, 'global' and 'local'. The global error is the type which affects the interpretation of the whole sentence, and the local error merely a part of it, a clause or a phrase. For example, the sentence 'The soldiers had been shooting when they are blindfolded' contains examples of both kinds of error. The major error, the one most likely to lead to misunderstanding of the sentence, is the substitution of 'shooting' for 'shot'. This error we can call global; it affects the interpretation of the entire sentence. The awkward present tense in the subordinate clause 'when they *are* blindfolded' constitutes a local

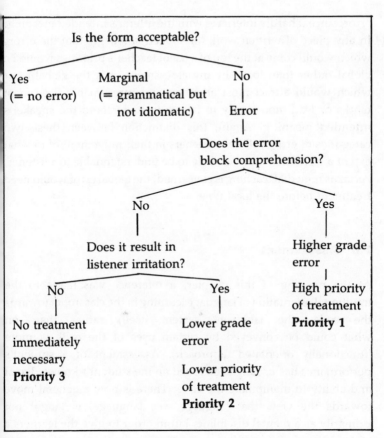

Figure 12

This diagram (adapted from Olsson 1973:) shows a method for working out an order of priority in dealing with errors. It is suggested that errors that cause irritation but do not block comprehension should receive a lower priority of treatment than those which prevent comprehension or mislead the listener. Teachers who are not native English speakers should, if in doubt, consult a native speaker or as many of their colleagues as possible on their ideas as to priorities two and three. Priority one should provide few problems.

error, since it hardly interferes with the utterer's intended meaning. In any piece of written work (or spoken language, too) the errors which would come at the top of a list of teacher's priorities would be global rather than local. In any assessment, it is the global error which would attract most attention and, presumably, lose most marks or lead more easily to failure to understand the speaker's intended meaning. Again, this distinction between these two categories of error will help teachers in their judgement of to what extent a learner's output is likely to be understandable to a listener. As far as remedial teaching is concerned, the global error would need treatment before the local type.

7.6 Assessment

At the opening of this chapter, a reference was made to the traditional orientation of language learning in the classroom towards the code (the language system itself) rather than on what could be conveyed by certain uses of the code (a more 'functionally orientated' approach). Assessment of a student's performance has usually been based on the student's knowledge of and ability to manipulate the code. There is now a general move towards the view that language, *any* language, is taught not primarily as a mental discipline, but in order to give the learners a tool to use for different purposes. This means that examining and testing will have to begin to move away from the traditional area of just the code and, instead, assess the uses that the learner can make of the code.

This is an area which is highly problematic, but work is going on in this field now (for instance, see Levine 1976, Morrow 1977 and in this series, Harrison 1983), seeking ways of assessing learners without necessarily penalising every deviation in the code. An extreme example of this approach to assessment can be found in Newmark (1971), where the criterion for 'passing' the test was the impression of a native language speaker that he had 'had a conversation' with the candidate, with whom he had been closeted face to face. This approach is hardly suited to major public examinations, and for the foreseeable future the large scale assessments that can be carried out are likely to remain as they are, with a focus on accuracy rather than fluency. There are, however, some exceptions. The University of Cambridge First Certificate in English examination includes a paper on 'situations' in which the student is assessed on his ability to communicate using appropriate language in different situations. See Figure 13 for examples of the type of question asked.

PAPER 5: SITUATIONS

1. You want to use a public telephone but don't know how. Ask someone near.

2. You want to book an airline ticket to New York, but the first plane is fully booked. What do you say?

3. You need to return to your own country or town unexpectedly in the middle of the school term. Ask for permission.

4. The television set you have rented isn't working. Ask at the shop for someone to repair it.

Figure 13

Teachers who are confident of their own ability to pick out the appropriate style can give students practice in this kind of work in class. An easier task may be to give an utterance as a stimulus and to get the pupils to pick out from a number of possible responses the most suitable one.

For example: 'Do you mind if I smoke?'
a   Oh, please do not.
b   I'd rather you didn't.
c   I would like you not to smoke.
d   You cannot smoke here.

The emphasis here would not be on the grammatical correctness, as they are all grammatical, but rather on matching a reply in the same style to the original request (b is the most appropriate).

As teachers become increasingly aware of an alternative order of priorities in teaching, so the attitude towards error will begin to change. Since error plays a major role in the breakdown of communication if it occurs too frequently, it is always going to be an area of language use which needs to be tested. The major disadvantage of an approach to assessment based on what the learners *cannot* do is that it orients classroom activities towards an approach too heavily dependent on accuracy, which in turn leads to the conditions described earlier in this chapter. Another tendency in assessing, related to this general orientation, is to choose those specific items for assessment which are known, possibly as the result of an error analysis, to be difficult for the learners. These may be exceptions to rules (sentences involving 'strong' verbs, irregular plural forms, etc) or particular forms in a target language which may be easily confused with forms in the mother tongue.

For example, in Amharic, the verb for 'visit' sounds very much like the English verb 'ask', and these words are confused. Then again, in German, the verb *bekommen* does not mean the same as the English word 'become' which sounds similar. This can be seen in the classic mistake of the German-speaking guide who tells his English tourists to 'Go round the corner and you will all become donkeys' (bekommen means 'receive' or 'get' in English). The English relative clause is another area which frequently causes problems in accuracy (although not necessarily in comprehensibility) with '....the man I saw *him* yesterday is a friend of mine'.

In the interests of obtaining a wide spread of marks, it is this type of item which is often chosen for assessment purposes. This in itself may be desirable, but what, in effect, does it tell us about the students who achieve high marks, or even low marks, in this kind of test? Experience shows us that students who get good marks cannot necessarily use their knowledge to communicate. Perhaps the ideal is a test which combines the material which will result in a wide range of marks — a 'difficult' test — with an activity to be assessed on more communicative grounds. This may be difficult to achieve in public examinations, but it could still be a goal in the classroom.

Summary

1 It is typical of students to be reluctant to make the most of an opportunity to use the language they are learning. This is because of a fear of appearing 'unintelligent'. This fear is brought about by demanding perfect accuracy before communicative activities are encouraged.

2 Making mistakes does not always mean that comprehensibility is lost but we cannot pretend that accuracy is totally unimportant. If too many mistakes are made, then the redundancy built into any language will not suffice. Both accuracy *and* fluency are important.

3 Errors in grammar are more likely to interfere with communication than inexact selection of vocabulary items, as are errors which affect the whole sentence rather than just part of it.

4 When marking a piece of written work, it may be useful to calculate the relative number of errors made in order to avoid the tendency to penalise a longer piece of writing for having more mistakes than a shorter one.

5 Ideally, language learners should be assessed not only according to what they have not learnt but also by giving them the opportunity to show what they can do with the language they are learning.

8 Implications and applications

This short final chapter contains little that has not already been discussed in the earlier chapters of this book. Its aim is rather to bring together in summary form the implications for the classroom language teacher of what has been said.

The overall approach of this book has reflected current thinking in the fields of psychology of errors, sociology of language and the linguistics of language teaching. If we are to stand any chance of improving our teaching of languages, we need in the first instance to know more about how learners actually go about learning languages; the study of their performance, the errors and mistakes *and* the correct forms may tell us something about this. The aim of this book is to bring to classroom teachers some of the recent ideas in this field. They may not all have direct applications in the classroom, but nearly all of the findings will have implications for language teaching methods.

8.1 Inevitability of errors

One of the main themes of this book is the virtual inevitability of error in learners' work. Not only is it almost inevitable, but there are strong reasons for believing it to be an essential part of learning, in that it aids the learner and provides him with feedback in the process of concept formation.

The implications of this are that learners should be given encouragement in the situation where errors arise when they attempt to express what they have not yet been taught to say. Disapproval should *on no account* be shown. There is a practical problem here that most language teachers will be aware of: that of grading the material. If the learner wishes to say something that will involve him in parts of the language which occur later in the book or course, should the teacher alter the plan and teach the relevant items earlier than intended? It would do no harm, if the items needed are not too far advanced in complexity, to give them to the learner(s) who need them, assuming there is adequate time.

There is no reason to alter the design of the course fundamentally and allowing the learner to express his information in a form he knows is correct is always encouraging. It may be that he will not remember or learn the language item as a result of this. On the other hand, he may. If not, then when the particular language items are introduced formally, he will be in a very much better position to learn them, since he will already have used them. Indeed, the 'spiral syllabus' is recommended by Corder (1973). In a spiral syllabus the same items recur in different uses and different complexities, so that, for example, the use of the present continuous tense in English to indicate future intention ('I'm going to Düsseldorf tomorrow morning') will not be included in the first entry of this tense into the course book or syllabus, but would occur later, so that forms are introduced and re-introduced with different functions.

If we encourage our learners to adopt a freer approach, at least orally, we shall not be encouraging them to progress 'too fast', to use language which is too difficult, but rather language which they may have a need for. Indeed, one approach to the language-learning business actually involves the learners in doing just this — determining their own language input depending on the subjects they wish to speak about with their fellow learners. It is known as 'community language learning' (Curran 1976).

Community language learning (CLL) involves a group of learners who sit in a circle with an informant who knows the target language. One member of the group speaks to another on a topic of interest.

The informant then whispers the target language version of what the learner has said. The learner then repeats the target language version, eventually recording it. In this way a conversation is built up. In the next stage, the grammar of the conversation is studied with the informant's assistance.

The practicalities of the average classroom will still necessitate a graded syllabus in the majority of cases. There is no reason why though, given the time, the teacher should not allow some time for activities which are not quite so controlled (see Revell 1979 for examples).

8.2 Correcting errors

Various suggestions have been made in this book about the problem of correction of errors once they have occurred. One view that has been expressed is the liberal view that correction as such may achieve very little. Tolerance should be encouraged, since correction and reteaching take up useful time which could be devoted to exposing the learner to more of the language, and that exposure itself may help the learner to a stage of interlanguage development which is closer to the target language than his present stage. Correction, in this liberal view, is seen as a waste of valuable time. However, constraints on this view have also been mentioned. These relate to the immediate practicalities of the classroom and include examination demands, often based on accuracy.

8.3 Errors in writing

Another point that has been made on the subject of error in written work is that ideally, students should not be in the position of producing a large number of incorrect written forms, since if they do, it is not psychologically rewarding for them, and it is costly in terms of the teacher's time and effort.

In this area at least, prevention is better than cure, from a purely practical perspective. On the occasions, however, when errors do creep through, it may be more useful to the learner to be able to treat the working out of exactly *what* is wrong as a kind of puzzle, with the aid of the teacher's coded indications. This approach involves the learner in more thought about the erroneous forms; the mechanical copying down of correct sentences has never been shown to have any lasting effect on learners. If the learner is involved intellectually with the activity, he is much more likely to learn from his experience.

Another suggestion that has been made about correction of written work is that from both the teacher's and the learner's point of view, correction of every single error is likely to be a waste of time. A wiser and more economical course is to concentrate on one particular area: the teaching point of the lesson or unit. Except in cases where a timely reminder may be necessary, the mistake can be ignored — it is the systematic error which is of interest, the rule which is not fully learnt or not known at all. In most cases, teachers are familiar with what their classes know — or at least, what they have been taught. As was remarked earlier, teaching and learning are, however, not *necessarily* related!

8.4 The correction of speech errors

On the subject of correcting the speech of our learners, a general guide might be stated as follows: when the learner is more concerned with expressing a meaning, imparting some information or opinion, than he is with the forms of language he is using for that purpose, he should not be stopped and corrected 'in mid-stream'. This is not to say that teachers need pay no attention to the student's manner of expressing the meaning, but that an actual stoppage would probably not be profitable.

If the teacher carries a small notebook to record the more general problems as he becomes aware of them, they can be incorporated into later teaching points, not necessarily as 'remedial' teaching, but as straightforward developmental teaching. If the material has been covered before at a lower level with only partial success, then the approach may need altering; if the previous treatment was structural, the mastery of the code of the language being the main aim, a more functional approach could be adopted, with the focus on various uses, or one particular use that the particular structure could be put to.

An example of this approach could be as follows. The teacher, faced with a new class, discovers that the past simple and continuous question forms have not been fully learnt. After some fairly traditional teaching, the class is prepared for an activity — the game 'Alibis' — which involves a lot of motivated use of these question forms.

Alibis

Members of the class divide into pairs and decide on an alibi to prove that they were not guilty of the crime that has been committed.

Two of the best students are chosen as the 'suspects'. They go outside and together make up a detailed story to account for their movements on the evening of the crime.

While they are outside, the teacher rehearses with the class the sort of questions they, representing the police, will put to the suspects on their return. The questions will be mainly in the past simple or continuous, for example, 'What did you do at . . .?' 'What were you doing at . . .?'

Then the first suspect is called in and the interrogation begins, as many pupils as possible asking a question. The teacher may help to make things clear. The second suspect is called in and interrogated, while the first one is sent out. The object is to expose contradictions in the two suspects' stories, for example, one may say he was sitting upstairs in the cinema, the other that they sat downstairs.

Re-questioning of each suspect soon reveals all the points of difference between their stories and the alibi breaks down. These points the teacher now discusses with the class, thus practising certain patterns of reported speech.

An activity such as this results in intense, enjoyable and thoroughly motivated practice of particular forms. The students' attention is focused much more on the use to which the code is being put than on the code as something to be learnt.

8.5 Different styles of language

A functional approach can also be used for correcting student's speech when their problem seems to be one of style. Comparisons can be drawn between different styles of conversation, structure and vocabulary items related to specific situations, an approach which Johnson and Morrow (1978, 1979) follow. Varying degrees of formality can be exemplified. For example, in the context, 'The manager asked the customer to . . . the restaurant', we could choose between the following: leave, get out of, quit, vacate. They would clearly not all be appropriate, but the choice would be partially determined by the context, the manner in which the manager was thought to be speaking, when and to whom. A manager of a transport cafe would not be likely to address his customers in the same way as the manager of an expensive restaurant. Similarly, a girl saying goodnight to her boyfriend is not likely to use the same kind of language as a guest taking his leave of hosts he does not know very well. As a further example, if the following two 'descriptions' (from Morrow and Johnson 1979:35, 137) are compared, it will be seen that they differ in a number of ways, notably in vocabulary and structure.

Talking about other people
On the tape you will hear descriptions of five people. You will hear:
A girl describing her fiancé.
A boy describing a girl he dislikes.

A writer describing a historical figure.

A police description of a criminal.

A friend describing his cousin whom you are going to meet.

i)   Listen to the tape. Which person is being described?

ii) Listen again. Fill in as much information as you can.

	Hair	Build	Height	Looks
1 Criminal				
2				
3				
4				
5				

People

i)   He is 37 years old, approximately 5' 8" tall with short black hair. He is well-built and extremely strong. This man is dangerous and may attack without warning. He should not be approached by members of the public.

ii) Oh she's a dreadful person. She's got lots of money, but she's really mean. She hates spending money. She's not very tall — about 5' and she's rather thin. I suppose she's got blond hair, but she's not at all attractive. That face! Oh, God! She's awful.

iii) She'll be at the station at 5.30. She's got long red hair and she's very good-looking. She's fairly tall — about 5' 8" and very slim. Yes, I'm sure you'll enjoy meeting her.

iv) What else can I say? He doesn't always agree with what I say, but he always listens to my opinions. He's really good-looking too — very tall, about 6' 2". He's slim and he's got lovely fair hair. Just the man for me.

v)   In appearance he was an imposing figure. About 6' tall with long fair hair, he left a lasting impression on everyone he met — especially women, who generally found him very good-looking. He was particularly known for his warm, friendly character. Whenever a friend was in trouble, he never failed to help.

Many writers of textbooks now are seeking to escape from the 'textbook English' which frequently in the past led to the learner's unawareness of the characteristic stylistic variations in English. These variations depend upon the speakers, *purpose* of speech and the situation where the language is used. What is true of spoken English is also true of letter-writing. For many years learners' attention has been drawn to the typical style of the business letter as compared with, say, a letter to a friend. What more recent textbooks are doing now is to develop this approach and use it in relation to dialogues and other uses of English. The problem here for the non-native-speaking teacher of English in treating this more subtle type of learner error is precisely that he or she may lack confidence in these matters. For this there can be only one remedy; exposure to as much English as used in different situations as possible. For many this may well mean listening to the BBC World Service or the Voice of America.

Both published and home-made tapes will also be useful. This is the type of material that teachers can usefully share with each other.

There is, however, no real substitute for experiencing the language spoken in the different situations in countries where English is a first language. On the other hand, in a second language environment, the problems are not so great, as the different styles can be directly experienced both by the teacher and the learner. In this type of environment, the styles used may differ considerably from those in the country where the language is the sole mother tongue. It is generally possible for teachers, if they wish, to acquire cassettes of different types of English which can be heard on the BBC World Service, and examples of different styles of the written language, either through friends, or an organisation such as The British Council or the United States Information Service. (Addresses can be found in the local telephone directory.)

8.6 Conclusion

It may seem anomalous to the reader that in a book which purports to be about learners' errors, the main point expressed throughout has been that teachers should learn to tolerate errors more, and even view them as inevitable, a view which may have been accepted by the more cynical teacher for some considerable time. Now there is a considerable body of evidence to show that although it is the case that errors are inevitable a language teacher need not resign himself to this fact with a shrug of the shoulders. Instead, errors can be accepted as an indication of some kind of learning activity taking place in the learner.

The learner, in a very real sense, must create his language for himself. The teacher cannot learn it for him. As von Humboldt put it, as long ago as 1836 (the idea is *not* a new one!) (*Die Sprache*) . . .*lässt sich, wenn es auch auf den ersten Blick anders erscheint, nicht eigentlich lehren, sondern nur im Gemüthe wecken; man kann ihr nur den Faden hingeben, an dem sie sich von selbst entwickelt.* (Language cannot actually be taught, although it may appear at first sight that it can. It can only be aroused in the mind, and be given the thread with which to develop itself.')

Bibliography

Abbott G, 'Intelligibility and Acceptability in Spoken and Written Communication' in English Language Teaching Journal, Vol 33 No 3 1979:168-76.

Bailey N, Madden C and Krashen S D, 'Is there a natural sequence in Adult Second Language Learning?' in Language Learning No 24 1974.

Burt M K and Kiparsky C, *The Gooficon: A Repair Manual for English*, (Newbury House, 1972).

Chomsky C, *The Acquisition of Syntax in Children from Five to Ten*, (MIT Press, 1969).

Cook V, 'Cognitive Processes in Second Language Learning' in International Review of Applied Linguistics Vol 15 No 1 1974:1-20.
English Topics, (Oxford University Press, 1974).
'The English are Only Human' in International Review of Applied Linguistics Vol 33 No 3 1979:163-8.

Corder S Pit, 'Idiosyncratic Dialects and Error Analysis' in International Review of Applied Linguistics Vol 9 No 2 1971:147-60.
Introducing Applied Linguistics, (Penguin, 1973).
Error Analysis, Interlanguage and Second Language Acquisition, Language Teaching and Linguistics Abstracts, Vol 8 No 4 1975.

Curran C A, *Counselling Learning In Second Languages*, (New York: Apple River Press, 1976).

Doughty P S, Pearce J and Thornton G, *Exploring Language*, (Edward Arnold, 1972).

Dulay H and Burt M, 'Natural Sequences in Child Second Language Acquisition' in Language Learning Vol 24 No 1 1974:37-53.

Etherton A R T S, 'Error Analysis – Problems and Procedures' in English Language Teaching Journal Vol 32 No 1 1977:67-78.

George H V, *101 Substition Tables for Students of English*, (Oxford University Press, 1967).

Common Errors in Language Learning, (Newbury House, 1972).

Greene J, *Thinking and Language*, (Methuen, 1975).

Harrison A, A Language Testing Handbook (Macmillan, 1983).

Hatch E, 'Acquisition of Syntax in a Second Language' in Richards (QV) 1978.

Hornby A S, *A Guide to Patterns and Usage in English*, (Oxford University Press, 1954).

Hudson G, *A Classification of Ethiopian Student Errors in English Essay Writing*, (mimeograph, University of Addis Ababa, 1971).

Humboldt W von, *Über die Verschiedenheit des menschlichen Sprachbaues*, (1836, Facsimile edition, Bonn, 1960).

James C, 'An Exculpation of Contrastive Linguistics' in Nickel G (Ed), *Papers in Contrastive Linguistics*, (Cambridge University Press, 1971).

Contrastive Analysis, (Longman, 1980).

Johnson K and Morrow K, *Approaches*, (Cambridge University Press, 1978, 1979).

Krashen S, *Second Language Acquisition and Second Language Learning* (Pergamon 1981)

Ladefoged P, *Three areas of Experimental Phonetics* (Oxford University Press, 1967)

Lenneberg E, 'Biological Foundations of Language' in Hospital Practice Dec. 1967:59-67.

Levine J, 'An Outline Proposal for Testing Communicative Competence' in English Language Teaching Journal Vol 30 No 2 1976:128-35.

Long M, *Face to Face*, (Evans, 1976).

Maley A and Duff A, *Drama Techniques in Language Learning*, (Cambridge University Press, 1978).

McDonough S, *Psychology in Foreign Language Teaching*, (Allen and Unwin, 1981).

McNeill D, 'Developmental Psycholinguistics' in Smith G and Miller G (Eds), *The Genesis of Language*, (MIT Press, 1966).

Moody K, *Written English Under Control*, (Oxford University Press, 1968).

Morrow K, *Techniques of Evaluation for a Notional Syllabus*, (Royal Society of Arts, 1977).

Nemser A, 'Approximative Systems of Foreign Language Learners' in International Review of Applied Linguistics Vol 9 No 2 1971:115-23.

Newmark L, 'A Minimal Language Teaching Programme' in Pimsleur P and Quinn T (Eds), *The Psychology of Second Language Learning*, (Cambridge University Press, 1971).

Olsson M, 'The Effects of Different Types of Errors in the Communication Situation' in Svartvik J (Ed), *Errata*, (Gleerup, 1973).

Pincas A, *Teaching English Writing* (Macmillan, 1982).

Politzer R L, 'An Experiment in the Presentation of Parallel and Contrasting Structures' in Language Learning
Vol 18 Nos 1 and 2.

Revell J, *Teaching Techniques for Communicative English*, (Macmillan, 1979).

Richards J, *Error Analysis*, (Longman, 1974).
Understanding Second and Foreign Language Learning:
Issues and Approaches, (Newbury House, 1978).

Rixon S, *How to Use Games in Language Teaching*, (Macmillan, 1981).

Selinker L, 'Interlanguage' in International Review of Applied Linguistics Vol 10 No 3 1972:219-31.

Skinner B F, *Verbal Behaviour*, (Appleton Century Crofts, 1957).

Smith N and Wilson D, in Journal of Linguistics No 3 1975.

Stevick E, *Memory, Meaning and Method*, (Newbury House, 1976).

Stockwell R P, Bowen J D and Martin J W, *The Grammatical Structures of English and Spanish*, (University of Chicago Press, 1965).

Stockwell R P and Bowen J D, *The Sounds of English and Spanish*, (University of Chicago Press, 1965).

Strutridge G and Geddes M, *Listening Links*, (Heinemann, 1978).

Tench P, *Pronunciation Skills*, (Macmillan, 1981).

Ure J, 'A Ghana Anthology with Bi-Lingual Exercises' in pilot edition, (University of Ghana, 1974).

Valdman A, 'Error Analysis and Pedagogical Ordering' in Corder S Pit and Roulet E (Eds), *Linguistic Insights in Applied Linguistics*, (Didier, 1975).

de Villiers P and J, *Early Language*, (Fontana, 1979).

Widdowson H G, *Reading and Thinking in English*, (Oxford University Press, 1980).

Glossary of linguistic terms

Cross-references are given in bold type.

accuracy	Emphasising correct grammar, as sometimes opposed to **fluency.**
ambiguity	Having at least two meanings, thus leaving the listener or reader in doubt as to the speaker's or writer's meaning and intention.
antecedent	Noun, phrase or clause to which a pronoun refers, for example *My father* who . . .,
appropriacy	Suitability of language for the situation in which it is used.
acquire	The natural process of getting a spoken language in everyday life, involving little or no conscious learning.
behaviourist	A school of psychology concerned primarily with the interpretation of behaviour as **habits.**
code	The systems (grammar, meaning and sound) of language
cognitive	Concerned with the thought processes.
collocation	The company a word keeps; the usual context of a word.
communication strategy	A procedure used by learners to convey their meaning; it may not be 'grammatical'.

community language learning	A way of learning a language in small groups using an informant and translation.
concept formation	Development of a mental picture, image or idea.
contrastive analysis	An activity which contrasts the grammatical, semantic and phonological systems of two or more languages.
covert (error)	An error which is not immediately apparent.
decode	To work out the meaning of an utterance by using knowledge of the **code**.
descriptive (rule)	A language ruled based not on what an authority believes language users **should** do, but on observation of what they actually do.
deviant structure	An 'incorrect' grammatical item.
diagnostic	Aimed at discovering the gaps in a learner's knowledge.
error	A systematic deviation from the accepted **code**.
extinction	The dying out of a **habit.**
false concept	An inaccurate idea about a (grammatical) rule.
fluency	Ease and confidence in using those parts of the **code** a learner has experienced.
fossilisation	Language behaviour becoming fixed at a certain point in development.
global error	An error which affects the meaning of the whole sentence.
habit theory	The theoretical ideas underlying **behaviourist** psychology.

hypothesis	An informed guess made with the help of given information.
interlanguage	The language used by the learner as he progresses from no knowledge at all of the **target language** to a satisfactory knowledge. The interlanguage is constantly changing.
interference from L₁	The effects of 'habits' formed in the speaker's first language acting upon the **target language**.
L₁,	First language (usually the **mother tongue**).
L₂	Second language **(Target Language)**.
L₁ transfer	Use of what the learner knows about his first language to try and assist expression in the **target language**.
lapse	A non-systematic deviation from the **code** due to human limitations such as fatigue, poor memory, etc.
learning strategies	Processes used by learners (eg **mnemonics)** to assist in learning.
lingua franca	A language used for communication by people with differing first languages in a given environment.
local error	An error which only affects the meaning of the clause in which it is found.
message	The meaning conveyed by the language **code**.
mistake	A non-systematic deviation from the language **code** indicating incomplete learning.
mnemonics	Devices to assist the memory (for example, memorising the sentence 'Read out your green book in verse' to remember the colours of the spectrum.)

mother tongue	First language.
non-defensive language behaviour	A learner's willingness to take risks when using the **target language**.
overt error	An immediately apparent error.
over-generalisation	A failure by the learner to apply restrictions where appropriate to the application of a rule.
peer checking	Other learners assisting in checking for errors or mistakes, usually in class.
performance analysis	An examination of both 'correct' and 'incorrect' forms used by learners.
redundancy	More information than is necessary to derive the **message** from the **code**.
redundancy reduction	A learner's removal of apparently unnecessary information in a language system (eg 'He *go* there yesterday').
regression	A movement backward to an earlier stage of learning; (in reading) a backward movement of the eye to cover material already looked at.
second language/ foreign language	A distinction often made between situations of language use: *second language* is where the language in question is used for some purpose(s) outside the classroom; *foreign language* is where the language is **not** used outside the classroom.
segmental	Relating to the phonemic sounds of a language, excluding stress and intonation.
spiral syllabus	A syllabus planned along structural lines, but involving systematic uses of those structures and constant revision.

stress timing	A pattern of regular stresses, irrespective of the number of unstressed syllables between them
suprasegmental	Relating to stress and intonation.
syllable timing	A pattern of syllables, each taking roughly the same amount of time.
target language	The language which the learner is learning.

Further reading

1 General

Burt M K and Kiparsky C, *The Gooficon: A Repair Manual for English*, (Newbury House, 1972). A useful and practical book detailing correction procedures. Based on the non-native language interference model.

Cook V J, 'The analogy between first and second language learning,' in IRAL (International Review of Applied Linguistics) 7 1969:207-16.

'The comparison of language development in native children and foreign adults,' IRAL 11 1973:13-28. Two early articles pointing out the similarities of the process of first and second language learning, with some practical suggestions for error treatment in the first.

Corder S Pit, *Introducing Applied Linguistics*, (Penguin, 1973). Useful all-round book for views on how linguistics impinges on language teaching. The section on error is useful for the distinction between 'errors' and 'mistakes'.

'Error Analysis, Interlanguage and Second Language Acquisition,' in Kinsella V (Ed) *Language Teaching and Linguistics: Surveys*, (CILT, British Council and Cambridge University Press, 1977.) A very useful survey of the field up to 1977. A compendious bibliography is a major feature of this article.

ELT Documents No.102, (The British Council, 1978). This volume contains a collection of papers dealing with the problems of local models and varieties of English in second as well as foreign language environments.

French F G, *Common Errors in English: their Cause, Prevention and Cure*, (Oxford University Press, 1949). A traditional statement of the view that errors are not desirable, but this is a book in which first language interference is *not* accorded pride of place.

George H V, *Common Errors in Language Learning*, (Newbury House, 1972). An early statement of the more liberal view of errors in learners' output. Useful on the topic of redundancy in language and the learner's tendency to reduce it.

Halliday M A K, *Learning How to Mean*, (Edward Arnold, 1975). Authoritative statement on the creation of language functions rather than structure.

Rivers W and Temperley M, *A Practical Guide to the Teaching of English*, (Oxford University Press, 1978). Precisely what it claims to be, with practical suggestions on teaching methods. Advice on the avoidance of unnecessary errors.

Schumann J and Stenson N, *New Frontiers in Second Language Learning*, (Newbury House, 1975). This book of readings contains some useful articles on the inter-language theory.

2 Psychological aspects of the error

Hatch E, (Ed) *Second Language Acquisition: A Book of Readings*, (Newbury House, 1978). A major source of recent empirical work on the process of second language acquisition, with studies on learners of all ages.

Richards J C, (Ed) *Error Analysis: Perspectives on Second Language Acquisition*, (Longman, 1974). Contains many of the pioneering papers in the area, including Selinker's on Interlanguage, the early Pit Corder papers, and Burt and Dulay on Goofing.

Understanding Second and Foreign Language Learning: Issues and Approaches, (Newbury House, 1978). Empirical and theoretical papers centring around the interlanguage theory.

Stevick E, *Memory, Meaning and Method*, (Newbury House, 1976). Totally absorbing personal statement, supported with evidence from empirical research, on the author's beliefs on the relation of these three variables and their relation to language learning.

de Villiers P and J, *Early Language,* (Fontana, 1979). Easily assimilable account of the latest ideas on first language acquisition. Contains a bibliography for those who wish to become more technical on the subject.

3 Testing and assessment

Davies A, (Ed) *Language Testing Symposium,* (Oxford University Press, 1968). Contains papers on both the theory of 'discrete point testing' (testing the 'code') and also some work on the problems of testing in a second language environment. Interesting paper by Keith Brown on 'Intelligibility'.

Lado R, *Language Testing,* (Longman, 1961). The classic book on the issues involved in testing the language code, firmly based in audio-lingual habit formation theory, and first language interference.

Levine J, 'An Outline Proposal for Testing Communicative Competence' in English Language Teaching Journal Vol 30 No 2 1976:128-35. An early article facing the problem of testing what learners can do with a language, rather than what they can do to the code. Useful short bibliography.

Morrow K, *Techniques of Evaluation for a Notional Syllabus,* (Royal Society of Arts, 1977). A monograph which attempts to come to terms with testing communicative functions. Practical suggestions and some theory. Useful, but expensive.

4 Error Analysis

Etherton A R B, 'Error Analysis: Problems and Procedures,' in English Language Teaching Journal Vol 32 No 1 1977:67-78. A short and very practical article on the techniques of setting up a small scale error analysis.

Index